CU00797322

DEAD
FAMOUS
LONDON

To the memory of …
Mal, Gordon, Michael and Vicki

© Jim Dyson 2013

PHOTOGRAPHY
All grave images, chapter images and cover © Jim Dyson / Getty Images 2008 - 2013
Archive headshots and map © Getty Images, except p42 courtesy of Twinings, p65 courtesy
of The FA and p153 courtesy of Liberty & Co.

Published by The Bluecoat Press, Liverpool
Printed in China by Latitude Press
Design by Gurjinder Bhandal-Dyson

ISBN 9781908457189

© All rights reserved. No part of this publication may be reproduced, stored in a retrieval
system, or transmitted in any form or by any means, electronic, mechanical, photocopying,
recording or otherwise, without prior permission from the publisher.

ACKNOWLEDGEMENTS
I would like to offer grateful thanks to Colin Wilkinson at Bluecoat Press and Rick
Mayston at Getty Images for their belief and continued support, as well as nods of
appreciation to my colleagues Dave Bruce, Bette Lynch & Stewart Stanley at Getty
Images. Thanks to Tom Hall for his boundless enthusiasm and company; Victoria
Ribbans & Duncan Jeffery at Westminster Abbey; Ian Dungavell at the Friends of
Highgate Cemetery Trust; Ed Holmes at St Pauls Cathedral; Eric Willis at Golders
Green Crematorium; Erica Wooff at St Lukes Charlton; Nicole and Gordon at St
Bartholomew the Great; Lynne Mullen at St Sepulchre; Oliver Ross at St Olaves;
The Parish Office at St Mary's Hendon and also to the legions of helpful staff
and volunteers in churches and cemeteries in and around the city. Thanks
also to Gurjinder, aka 'the wife', for her love, patience and support.

Cover image - St Patrick's Roman Catholic Cemetery, Leytonstone

deadfamouslondon.co.uk
facebook.com/DeadFamousLondon
twitter.com/DeadFamousLDN

gettyimages **BLUECOAT**

DEAD FAMOUS LONDON

Photography and text
Jim Dyson

THE BLUECOAT PRESS

The Hardy Tree, St Pancras Old Church

CONTENTS

'The boast of heraldry, the pomp of power,
And all that beauty, all that wealth e'er gave,
Awaits alike the inevitable hour.
The paths of glory lead but to the grave.'

Thomas Gray (1751)

DEAD FAMOUS LONDON

INTRODUCTION

Famous graves hold a unique fascination. Anyone with a passing interest in history can stand beside the actual resting place of some of history's most notable figures. Not just people you may have learned about in history classes at school, kings and queens and the like, but real and tangible figures who have not only altered the course of British history, but have shaped the future of mankind.

I can't really tell where this interest in graves came from; I suppose we all have an element of morbid fascination in us, but the appeal for me was primarily photographic. London's burial grounds are wonderful places to while away some time, sanctuaries of calm and reflection where we can escape the hustle of city life and engage in some top level celebrity spotting, dead ones of course. Long before moving to London I had visited Highgate Cemetery, it having long haunted my imagination, and it was in itself something of a pilgrimage. Years later, when I lived near to Highgate, my visits would be no less compelling.

The sheer extent of London's social history is so vast that it could not be sufficiently told in a thousand books. This book therefore is by no means definitive; Westminster Abbey alone is the country's largest mausoleum containing over 3000 burials, of these I have featured just eight. There are more authoritative guidebooks available, listing thousands of burials, most of which neither you nor I have ever heard of. Although these have proved useful in my research I didn't find them quite as interesting as I hope you find *Dead Famous*. I have simply attempted to provide a broad sweep across the capital's more significant characters, as well as those with whom we should be better acquainted, to bring us closer to the individuals that have shaped our lives. Some have made a significant contribution to the arts, others may have been fundamental in bringing about social or scientific change, the impact of which has spread far beyond British shores, but every one has a story to tell.

There were a few criteria for inclusion ... 1) I must have heard of them, and if I wasn't aware of them prior to research they must hold a distinct or unique interest to be included, such as Aphra Behn or Mary Seacole, 2) They must be interesting and 3) There should be a physical resting place, marked with a grave or monument of some sort, which can be photographed.

It can be a daunting challenge when faced with a cemetery packed with thousands of graves, and a real sense of discovery to find the one you're looking for. This was all part of the fun for me and as such I have not included maps with locations of graves as I don't want to spoil your fun should you wish to go hunting yourself.

I have found that there are few pleasures greater than picking your way through an overgrown cemetery in glorious isolation after a night of heavy snowfall, or driving on a late spring afternoon, to the accompaniment of David Bowie's *Hunky Dory*, in search of a forgotten corner of the English countryside. This book has given me enormous pleasure to compile and I hope it goes some way to inspiring a few experiences of your own.

Jim Dyson ◆ London 2013

Circle of Lebanon, Highgate Cemetery

NORTH
LONDON

SINGAPORE SLING

SIR THOMAS STAMFORD BINGLEY RAFFLES (d 1826)

Stamford Raffles was born on board a ship off the coast of Jamaica in 1781. He began working for the East India Company as a clerk at the age of 14 and in 1805 was posted to Penang, Malaysia, where he began a long and fruitful association with South-East Asia. Raffles excelled in learning the Malay language, which made him an invaluable asset to his colonial chiefs and he rose rapidly through the ranks.

In 1811 Raffles was installed as Lieutenant-Governor of Java. He opposed the slavery and opium trades, subjugated many kingdoms to British colonial rule and introduced a form of government under which the country prospered. He also established the British system of driving on the left that still applies in Indonesia today.

The British East India Company at the time was administered from Penang, but they felt they were losing trade to the Dutch who controlled the Dutch East Indies (Indonesia). So Raffles focused his attention on the little used yet potentially strategic island of Singapura on the southern tip of Malaysia (Singa, meaning 'Lion' in Sanskrit, and 'Pura' meaning city; the Lion City). The Dutch hadn't colonised this small island and so Raffles forged a treaty with the Sultan of Johor to set up a British colony and trading post, establishing Singapore as a free port in 1819.

Singapore became the gateway to the economic markets of the East, and remains to this day one of the world's busiest ports. Raffles drafted the city's first constitution in 1823; he outlawed slavery, established schools in the native languages and set up a magistrate and police force. The combination of a hardworking and diverse, multi-ethnic workforce, and a western constitution based on sound principles, brought about a more disciplined approach to business. Modern Singapore sustains a population of more than five million people, 40% of whom are foreigners, and is highly regarded as the freest and least corrupt economy in the world.

Stamford Raffles spent much of his time in South East Asia studying natural history, collecting specimens and describing more than 30 new species of bird and 13 species of mammal. There are even species that have been named in his honour, including the Red-crowned Barbet (Megalaima Rafflesi) and the Latticed Butterflyfish (Chaetodon Rafflesi), but most significantly the Rafflesia, a genus of parasitic plants that produce the world's largest flowers. It is also said that he kept a honey bear cub as a pet, which often joined him and his family for dinner.

When Raffles finally returned to England he founded the world's first scientific zoo, the Zoological Society of London in 1825, and became its first President. London Zoo eventually opened to the public in 1847, and today boasts a collection of more than 750 species of animals.

Raffles died suddenly from a stroke at his North London home, Highwood House, the day before his forty-fifth birthday. He was buried at St Mary's Church in Hendon, but the vicar, Theodor Williams, who had made his money investing in the slave trade, refused to allow Raffles' interment inside the church, such was his opposition to slavery.

In a subtle twist of fate Raffles came in from the cold when the church was extended in the 1920s, his tomb, originally against the exterior south wall of the church, is now situated in front of the high altar. Raffles is also memorialised in Westminster Abbey and at his original landing site on the bank of Singapore River with life-sized white marble sculptures.

A PORTRAIT OF ENGLAND

JOHN CONSTABLE (d 1837)

The great British romantic landscape artist John Constable grew up in rural Suffolk and although he lived most of his adult life in London he would spend his summers sketching and painting in Dedham Vale, reliving his boyhood on the banks of the Stour, and his winters creating ambitious six-foot canvases in his Hampstead studio.

As the 18th century was drawing to a close, the fashionable artists of the period were painting biblical portraits and neo-classical panoramas, relegating the landscape elements of a composition to the background. But Constable brought the landscape to the fore and chose to paint his directly from nature as a poetic expression, 'nature is the fountain's head, the source from whence all originality must spring'. By painting 'in situ' Constable would pre-suppose the vision of the Pre-Raphaelites' 'truth of nature', and ultimately he became a great influence on the French Romantics, as well as Impressionists such as Monet.

Constable was pre-occupied with the changing of light and its subtle effects on a scene; he made sketches of clouds and sky-scapes, recording the atmospheric conditions with an almost scientific attention to detail. His studies were greatly influenced by the work of ground-breaking amateur meteorologist Luke Howard, who had recently begun to classify cloud formations.

Constable's contemporaries at the Royal Academy deemed his visionary canvases unfashionable, and in his lifetime he sold only 20 paintings in England. His most famous painting, 'The Hay Wain' (1821), is now considered one of the nation's best-loved works of art, but was largely ignored by the British art establishment at the time. The romantic pastoral scene, depicting a horse drawn cart standing in the water at Flatford Mill on the River Stour, evokes the timeless spirit and tranquillity of rustic life, and later won him a gold medal from King Charles X when it was exhibited at the Paris Salon in 1824. Constable always found an appreciative audience in France and sold many more paintings there, although he refused to travel to promote his work, stating, "I would rather be a poor man (in England) than a rich man abroad".

In 1828 Constable's beloved wife Maria succumbed to tuberculosis following a protracted illness, leaving him to raise their seven children alone. In his considerable grief he wrote, 'Hourly do I feel the loss of my departed angel … I shall never feel again as I have felt'.

His contribution to British art was eventually recognised the following year and he was accepted into the Royal Academy, but only by a majority of one vote. Constable died at his home in Bloomsbury in 1837 of what appears to have been chronic indigestion, and was buried with his wife in a railed chest tomb in the churchyard of St John at Hampstead.

The area around Dedham Vale, which has come to exemplify the English countryside, is now more popularly referred to as 'Constable Country' and Flatford Mill, which was taken over by the National Trust in 1943, exists as a major tourist attraction. Visitors make the pilgrimage, not only to explore the countryside that inspired the great artist, but also to stand on the exact spot that Constable occupied with his easel when painting his masterpiece and find that the scene has little changed in nearly 200 years.

GRAVE SACRIFICE
ELIZABETH SIDDAL (d 1862)

The Rossetti grave at Highgate Cemetery is known for various reasons; first and foremost it is the resting place of the notable Victorian family; the patriarch Gabriel Rossetti, an Italian political exile, his wife Frances Polidori (the sister of John Polidori, author of the first English vampire story), and his gifted children, the poet Christina and writer William. Although this is not where the most famous child is to be found; the artist, poet and leader of the Pre-Raphaelite Brotherhood, Dante Gabriel Rossetti is buried in Birchington, Kent, but it is here with his family in Highgate that Dante's wife and muse Elizabeth Siddal was buried following her tragically young death. It is the tale of Dante and Siddal that has earned the Rossetti grave its rather macabre place in history.

Rossetti met young 'Lizzie' Siddal in 1849 when she was working as a milliner and artist's model. Siddal began to sit for the Pre-Raphaelites but Rossetti was captivated by her flawless complexion and flowing red hair. He jealously guarded his muse, even from his Pre-Raphaelite colleagues, and within two years she sat almost exclusively for him. The two were inseparable and soon became engaged. Rossetti painted her extensively and, under his tutelage, she became a respected artist in her own right.

Rossetti's sister Christina described their relationship in her poem 'In an Artist's Studio': 'One face looks out from all his canvases... He feeds upon her face by day and night, And she with true kind eyes looks back on him, Fair as the moon and joyful as the light.'

Siddal suffered from long-term ill health, which she countered by becoming addicted to Laudanum, an opium based tincture that proved popular amongst the Victorian bohemian set. In 1860 she and Rossetti married in private at a church in the Sussex town of Hastings, but just two years later, at the age of 32, Siddal died from an opiate overdose.

It has been suggested that Siddal took her own life and left a suicide note for Rossetti's attention; he is said to have had it destroyed in order to protect her character and possibly his own guilt for having an affair. Rossetti was so consumed by grief he made a gesture of sacrifice and love at his wife's graveside and placed his notebook of poetry in the coffin before it was sealed.

Rossetti's career began to stall in the years that followed and he all but stopped writing poetry. Some of his contemporaries however had achieved fame by publishing collections of romantic poetry; Rossetti was compelled to do the same but most of his original work had been buried at Highgate. He struggled with his conscience until a decision was made to recover the notebook.

Approval was granted and the exhumation was organised by Rossetti's literary agent Charles Howell, but Rossetti himself could not bear to attend and it was carried out in the dead of night with the utmost secrecy. Siddal's coffin was opened and the book was retrieved in reasonable condition, though some pages had been rendered unreadable by a worm hole.

When reporting back to Rossetti Howell told him that after seven years in the ground his wife's beauty had been immaculately preserved, she had suffered no decomposition and also that her famous red hair had continued to grow after death, filling the coffin. Word of this miraculous occurrence caused quite a stir, but given the state of the notebook, it is clear that Howell, a disreputable character at the best of times, had embellished his tale of the exhumation, not only for the sake of Rossetti's sanity but, if Rossetti had been too upset by the whole episode he may have less inclined to publish the works.

ELECTRIC DREAMS

MICHAEL FARADAY (d 1867)

The pursuit of science was always very much the preserve of the privileged upper classes and history's most eminent scientists have invariably been well educated and wealthy, but from very humble beginnings Michael Faraday made discoveries that would change the shape of the modern world. Faraday was born in the village of Newington Butts, south of London, roughly where Elephant and Castle is today, and there was nothing extraordinary about his upbringing; he was the son of a blacksmith, received only a rudimentary education and became an apprentice bookbinder.

Faraday's first taste of science came at the age of 20 when he was given tickets to attend a series of lectures at the Royal Institution by the celebrated chemist Humphry Davy. Faraday made extensive notes on Davy's observations and bound them together in a volume which he sent to Davy. Faraday was very conscious that he did not possess the breeding necessary to become a gentleman scientist but regardless he applied to Davy for a job and, after an initial rejection, he was employed as his assistant in 1813.

Following Davy's retirement in 1827 Faraday replaced him as Professor of Chemistry at the Royal Institution. It has been said that although Humphry Davy discovered many things his greatest discovery was Michael Faraday.

Faraday made experiments on the diffusion of gases, discovered the petrochemical compound Benzene, invented an early form of Bunsen burner and produced new kinds of optical glass, but his most important work was in the fields of electricity and magnetism.

As far back as 1600, when the personal physician to Queen Elizabeth I, William Gilbert, first coined the term 'electricity', there have been numerous breakthroughs in its discovery, from Benjamin Franklin's lightning experiments to Alessandro Volta's first battery. Faraday made pioneering experiments into the relationship between electricity and magnetism. In 1821 he found that a wire carrying an electric current would rotate around a magnet and from this motion he developed the principle of the modern electric motor, and in 1831 he invented the transformer which would go on to enable the transmission of high voltage electrical current. Although Faraday never concerned himself with the practical uses of electricity, both discoveries were crucial in harnessing the power of electricity as a potent new technology for a modern age.

Faraday's other great legacy was to start the Royal Institution Christmas Lectures in 1825, which were aimed at young people and sought to teach science in an entertaining way. These have been televised every year since 1966.

During the Crimean war Faraday was approached by the British government to advise on the production of chemical weapons, but he refused to co-operate, such was his moral objection. For the last 30 years of his life Faraday served as the scientific adviser to Trinity House, the home of the Lighthouse Authority, and as a gesture of thanks Prince Albert made the gift of a 'grace and favour' house at Hampton Court where he lived out his retirement.

Despite his ordinary upbringing Faraday became one of the most eminent scientists of the age. He refused a knighthood and also turned down the offer of a prestigious burial at Westminster Abbey. Instead Faraday was buried at Highgate Cemetery's dissenters plot, beneath a huge headstone, which at more than two metres tall even towers over the perimeter wall. In 1931 he was honoured with a memorial floor stone in the nave of Westminster Abbey, close to the grave of Sir Isaac Newton.

COMMUNIST PLOT
KARL MARX (d 1883)

Ask anyone to name a famous grave in London and they will invariably respond with that of Karl Marx, who appears to have become as famous for his grade I listed tomb at Highgate cemetery as for his revolutionary political philosophy.

In August 1844 Marx met his lifelong collaborator, the German socialist Friedrich Engels, in a Paris café. Marx was expelled from France for his radical activism and the two men convened in Brussels where they published the hugely influential *Communist Manifesto* in 1848. The manifesto defined the class struggle faced by the working proletariat, who were exploited by their bourgeois rulers, but who would ultimately rise to power through revolution. This potent ideology was the spur for what became known as the 'Spring of Nations' a wave of revolutions that spread across most of Europe that same year.

Marx moved to London in 1849 as a political exile with his wife Jenny and four children, where they were forced to live in extreme poverty for some years on Soho's Dean Street. Although he received financial assistance from Engels, the conditions were so bad that poor health claimed the lives of two of his children. He remained politically active however, and he and Engels attended meetings of the 'Communist League' at the Red Lion pub on Great Windmill Street, and Marx was even known to address crowds of onlookers from a soapbox at Speaker's Corner in Hyde Park.

Marx spent many years visiting the Reading Room at the British Museum where he carried out extensive political research for his most famous work, a critical analysis of the political economy of Capitalism, more popularly known as *Das Kapital*. The first volume was published in 1867 and later volumes were edited by Engels from Marx's notes, translations were made following Marx's death and the concept of Marxism proliferated. The 20th century saw a turbulent rise and fall in Communism but yet, early in the 21st century as Capitalism appears to be in global crisis, Marxism seems to be having something of a revival.

Marx's funeral was attended by just eleven people; he was buried in a modest plot in Highgate's East Cemetery with his wife, approximately 100 yards away from his present position. But the burial site became such a popular point of pilgrimage that a more fitting memorial was commissioned by the Communist Party of Great Britain in 1954. Liverpool artist and lifelong Socialist, Laurence Bradshaw, was awarded the great honour of designing Marx's iconic new monument. His striking bronze bust presents Marx as a powerful leader and the simple modernist marble pedestal bears the famous Communist rallying cry, 'Workers of all lands unite'.

Engels paid tribute to Marx at his funeral, "On the 14th of March, at a quarter to three in the afternoon, the greatest living thinker ceased to think. We found him in his armchair, peacefully gone to sleep, but for ever." He went on to describe his friend's death as "An immeasurable loss by the militant proletariat of Europe and America". Engels himself was cremated in 1895 and, at his request, his ashes were scattered off the cliffs at Beachy Head near Eastbourne.

Marx's ideologies will always be divisive and as a result his tomb is likely to receive a degree of unwelcome attention, but in January 1970 an attempt was made to bomb Marx's grave with a crude yet potent explosive device. Vandals tried to make a hole in the hollow bust into which they would fit the bomb, but they failed to cut through Marx's nose and the resulting explosion nearby caused minimal damage. It would appear that Marx remains as hard-headed in death as he was in life.

MURDER MOST INFAMOUS
CORA CRIPPEN (d 1910)

The case of Dr Crippen remains one of the most infamous in British legal history. The high profile case of 1910 caused an international sensation in its day; not only was this a story of murder, drama and suspense, but it was the first trial by media, the first arrest brought about by wireless radio communication and the first major conviction based on forensic evidence.

Hawley Harvey Crippen was a seemingly mild mannered homeopathic doctor from Michigan. He and his wife Cora moved to London in 1900. Cora was a flamboyant music hall actress, going by the stage name of 'Belle Elmore', but she enjoyed little success in show business. Whilst working as the manager of a medicine company on Oxford Street Dr Crippen fell in love with a typist by the name of Ethel Le Neve and they began an affair.

The Crippens held a dinner party on 31 January 1910 at their Camden home, 39 Hilldrop Crescent. The next day Cora had mysteriously disappeared. Crippen told friends and neighbours that she had returned to the United States. Not long after, his mistress moved in. The Music Hall Ladies Guild received a letter, supposedly from Cora, resigning her position as treasurer as she was leaving for the United States to visit relatives. A suspicious friend contacted the police with concerns about the nature of Cora's disappearance.

Detectives questioned Crippen at home and conducted a brief search, finding nothing untoward. When they returned a few days later Crippen and Le Neve had absconded. Police searched the house a further three times, eventually discovering mutilated human remains under the cellar floor. The cadaver's head, limbs, and skeleton were not found.

Wanted notices for Crippen and Le Neve were circulated and picked up by the international press who began to follow the case closely, fervently reporting each and every development. The keen eyed captain of the SS Montrose, a transatlantic ocean liner bound for Canada, noticed a father and son acting affectionately and recognised them as the fugitives in disguise.

Wireless telegraph technology, a very modern invention known as the Marconigram, was used to relay a message from the Montrose via The Daily Mail to police at Scotland Yard. Detectives boarded a fast ship and made chase across the Atlantic. London newspapers began preparing special editions in anticipation of the inevitable arrest.

The majority of the evidence against Crippen was circumstantial but it was the groundbreaking work carried out by pathologist Sir Bernard Spilsbury, the 'Father of Forensics', which brought about the guilty verdict. Spilsbury identified a scar on the torso of the victim that corresponded to an operation that Cora had undergone.

Dr Crippen was convicted of his wife's murder at the Old Bailey, the jury returning their verdict in less than half an hour. He was hanged at Pentonville prison on 23 November 1910 and buried with a photograph of his mistress in an unmarked grave. The women of the Music Hall Guild arranged a funeral for Cora in October, interring her remains in a grave at Islington & St Pancras Cemetery.

What had always appeared an open and shut case was re-examined in 2007 when an American forensic scientist used DNA profiling to ascertain that the remains found in the basement were not those of Cora. In fact the research suggests that it was the torso of a male. Although this throws the original conviction into doubt, and forces us to question who might actually be buried in Cora's grave, the inconclusive findings remain disputed and have not been substantiated by a court.

KING OF THE VAMPIRES
BRAM STOKER (d 1912)

Abraham Stoker began his writing career as a theatre critic, but is chiefly remembered for producing one of the most significant and definitive gothic horror stories of all time.

Following a complimentary review Stoker gave for a production of *Hamlet* in Dublin, he became close friends with its star Sir Henry Irving, the most celebrated actor of his time. Irving employed Stoker as an assistant and asked him to move to London to manage the Lyceum Theatre, a post he held for almost 30 years. London suited Stoker and he enjoyed the high life, mixing with the likes of Oscar Wilde and Conan Doyle; he was well acquainted with Prime Minister William Gladstone and even with two American Presidents.

It was during this time that Stoker would supplement his income by writing novels and short stories. *Dracula* was but one of many. Stoker researched his vampire book extensively, drawing from contemporary literature and historic folklore. The first apparent vampire in literature was John Polidori's Lord Ruthven in *The Vampyre*, published in 1819. The next significant addition to the genre was *Varney the Vampyre* in 1847, a work of cheap, sensational fiction, known as a penny dreadful. Stoker originally named his character 'Count Wampyr', and the Count's aristocratic mannerisms were largely based on his employer, Irving.

Whilst holidaying in Yorkshire, in 1890, Stoker visited Whitby library and happened upon a memoir by a former British consul, which outlined the history of the Wallachia region of Romania. A section detailing the 15th century Prince Voivode Dracula caught his eye; also known as Vlad Dracul, meaning 'devil' in the Wallachian language. It is thought that had Stoker known this was also the dreaded Vlad the Impaler, a brutal murderer responsible for tens of thousands of terrible deaths by impalement, he would surely have included some reference to this in his novel.

Dracula was published in 1897 to favourable reviews, but the enduring legend of his masterpiece and its enormous success came posthumously for Stoker.

The legions of 20th century interpretations began with *Nosferatu* a silent German film of 1922. Stoker's widow successfully sued the filmmakers as they had not sought permission or provided any royalties. Although she demanded the destruction of the film's negative and prints, copies survived and it remains an enduringly popular classic of early cinema. The first official filmed adaptation of *Dracula* came in 1931 and starred the great Bela Lugosi in a defining role. Dracula has since become the most portrayed horror character in cinematic history.

Bram Stoker died in 1912, following a series of strokes, unaware of the impact his book would have on the world. His ashes reside, rather fittingly, in the spooky, gothic surroundings of the Eastern columbarium at Golders Green Crematorium.

SOUP, SOAP & SALVATION
WILLIAM BOOTH (d 1912)

One of North London's best-kept secrets, set among 32 acres in Stoke Newington, is the charming cemetery of Abney Park. Established in 1840 as one of the capital's 'magnificent seven' municipal cemeteries, Abney Park catered for those who chose not to conform to the doctrines of the Church of England. The most prominent of these 'dissenters' was the Methodist preacher and humanitarian, William Booth.

Booth began his early career in Nottingham as an apprentice pawnbroker but, disturbed by the extreme poverty he saw many of his clients suffer; he took up evangelism as a means of reaching out to those less fortunate.

On completing his apprenticeship Booth moved to London and became a Methodist preacher. He met Catherine Mumford at a prayer meeting and they married in July 1855. Together they established the Christian Mission in the East End in 1865 to help society's desperate and impoverished. As William converted the poor to Christianity, Catherine gained financial support from the wealthy, and their charitable mission gradually expanded to 27 sites.

Booth was always keen to innovate though, and in 1878, in an effort to invigorate his cause, he renamed his volunteer workforce 'The Salvation Army'. Uniforms, marching bands and a system of military ranking were introduced, with Booth himself becoming the Army's first 'General'.

At a time when Victorian England was engaged in a series of colonial overseas wars, the idea of God's Army, battling sin with salvation, captured the public's imagination and the organisation grew rapidly, allowing Booth and his adherents to bring repentance and relief to many more thousands. Within just a few years the Army had expanded to North America and Australia.

During his 47 years of dedicated service Booth toured the world extensively, holding Salvationist meetings wherever he went and, in the process, he established the Army in 58 countries. During his ministry it is suggested that he travelled some five million miles. The stamina and belief of the man was inspirational; in 1904, and at the age of 75, Booth undertook the first of his motor tours from Land's End to Aberdeen in 29 days, during which time he spoke at 164 meetings. He created the template for many social welfare schemes and, by allowing women equal rights; he also promoted the women's suffrage movement, suggesting, "Some of my best men are women".

General William Booth passed away on 20 August 1912. Such was the outpouring of grief that 150,000 people passed by his coffin during the three days he lay in state at Clapton Congress Hall. The eldest of Booth's eight children and newly appointed 2nd General, Bramwell, conducted a memorial service in front of 35,000 mourners at Kensington Olympia, during which he described his father as "the happiest man I ever knew … a glad spirit". His impressive grave at Abney Park takes the shape of the Salvation Army shield.

With more than 1.5 million employees or 'soldiers', across 15,000 outposts, in 118 countries, speaking 175 languages, from soup kitchens to disaster relief, the Salvation Army remains a powerful force for good in the world as a charitable, international humanitarian agency.

PRIMA BALLERINA
ANNA PAVLOVA (d 1931)

Watching her first ballet at the age of eight a spellbound young girl from St Petersburg realised her vocation in life; she would become the most acclaimed ballerina in history.

Anna Pavlova wasn't naturally built for ballet though, she contended with weak ankles, long limbs and arched feet, struggling with her technique throughout ballet school. To combat the discomfort she suffered while dancing Pavlova began to modify her 'pointe' ballet shoes by hardening the toe and strengthening the sole for extra support. At the time this was enough for her to be branded a cheat, but she has since found credit as the originator of the modern pointe shoe. The more her fellow students taunted her, the greater her determination grew. She took extra tuition and practised relentlessly, eventually rising to become prima ballerina with the Imperial Russian Ballet in 1906 at St Petersburg's Mariinsky Theatre. Pavlova had become a star.

In 1911 London's Victoria Palace theatre hosted Pavlova's first British performance. The theatre's owner Sir Alfred Butt signalled his devotion to the ballerina by erecting a gilded statue atop the Palace roof. Pavlova treated this superstitiously however and she refused to look upon the likeness. The statue remained in place until 1939 when it was removed for safety, eventually disappearing altogether. It is presumed that the metal was used for the war effort. A replica took its place in 2006 where it can be seen today.

As Pavlova toured across Europe, and to America, audiences flocked to see the graceful styling of her classical performances. But in 1914 Germany declared war on her native Russia; she chose not to return and spent the rest of her life on tour making it her mission to bring ballet to the world. In the days before regular commercial aviation her extensive travels took her an estimated 350,000 miles in 15 years, watched by millions of adoring fans along the way. Her performances centred on the classics, which included 'The Sleeping Beauty' and 'Giselle' but she will always be remembered for her signature dance as 'The Dying Swan'.

Some time between 1926-29, whilst she toured Australia and New Zealand, the meringue and fruit dessert that bears her name, originally designed to represent a tutu, was first made in Pavlova's honour. The two countries have hotly disputed the origin of its creation ever since, although the earliest sources credit a chef in Wellington.

When travelling by rail in the Netherlands in 1931, Pavlova's train derailed. Dressed only in pyjamas she went out into the cold night to see what had happened. She died of pneumonia three weeks later at the age of 49. It is reputed that on her deathbed her dying words were to ask for her swan costume to be prepared. Pavlova was cremated at Golders Green Crematorium close to 'Ivy House', the home she kept in Hampstead.

Anna Pavlova's final curtain call came in 2001 when an attempt was made by the Mayor of Moscow to transfer her remains to the city's Novodevichy Cemetery to satisfy a clause in the will of her partner Victor Dandre. After much controversy, and at the very last minute, the Russian authorities refused permission to transport the urn. Her ashes remain pride of place in the Ernest George columbarium at Golders Green.

ANALYSE THIS

SIGMUND FREUD (d 1939)

Sigmund Freud was forced to emigrate from his Austrian homeland in 1938, but spent only 15 months living in exile in London before his death. He was the founder of psychoanalysis and is regarded as one of the most influential minds of the 20th century.

Freud revolutionised our understanding of what it means to be ourselves. He analysed the unconscious desires of the mind and developed the idea of 'Dream Interpretation' as wish fulfilment; he was an early proponent of the 'talking cure' and wrote extensively on the subject of psychiatry, putting forward many radical theories including the psychosexual development of children and the 'Oedipus complex'.

Freud developed a greater understanding of the conflicts that occur in the subconscious, and how they affect the behaviour of the individual, by dividing the functions of the mind into three distinct parts, he called the id (instinct), ego (reality) and super-ego (morality). He transformed the treatment of mental illness and created the language of psychiatry, which has proved so pervasive that we even refer to an unconscious slip of the tongue as 'Freudian'.

In 1923 Freud contracted oral cancer due, in no small part, to his lifelong passion for smoking up to 20 cigars a day. He underwent more than 30 operations and even had to be fitted with a prosthetic jaw, such was the extent of the damage his illness had caused him.

Freud was an old man when German troops occupied Austria and annexed the country to Nazi rule in 1938. At first he underestimated the threat of anti-Semitism and wished to remain in Vienna, but it was only when his daughter Anna was detained by the Gestapo and the family were put under house arrest that Freud was finally convinced to leave the country. Negotiations with the Nazi authorities proved to be difficult and he was forced to seek the help of a wealthy and influential former patient, Princess Marie Bonaparte, the great-grandniece of Emperor Napoleon I. Although she was able to help Freud and his immediate family, despite her best efforts she was not able to secure the escape of Freud's four sisters, who were in their seventies, and they eventually perished in Nazi concentration camps.

Freud left Vienna with his wife and daughter on the Orient Express bound for London, where he settled in Hampstead in very poor health. In the face of continued advice and appeals from doctors and family Freud never stopped smoking cigars and in September 1939, just weeks after war had been declared across Europe, he decided that he had suffered long enough and asked his doctor to assist in his 'suicide' by administering an overdose of morphine.

Freud's funeral was held at Golders Green Crematorium; his ashes were interred in an ancient Greek urn that had been gifted to him by his admirer Marie Bonaparte which was placed in a recess on a black marble column in the Ernest George columbarium. He was later joined by his wife Martha and is surrounded by the caskets of successive generations of the Freud family.

Anna Freud continued to live in the family's Hampstead home following her father's death and there she continued her father's work becoming a respected psychoanalyst herself, especially in the treatment of children. Following her death the house become a museum in honour of her father.

The Freud dynasty has continued to produce many more eminent members, from his grandchildren, the politician and chef, Sir Clement Freud and the artist Lucian Freud, the most successful painter of his generation, to his great grandchildren that include the broadcaster Emma Freud, who is married to the film director and 'Comic Relief' founder Richard Curtis, PR guru Matthew Freud, fashion designer Bella Freud, artist Jane McAdam Freud, novelist Esther Freud and businessman and politician Sir David, Baron Freud.

20th CENTURY BOY

MARC BOLAN (d 1977)

Marc Bolan was the brightest star of the glam rock scene of the seventies and a glittering career was sadly cut short with his untimely death a fortnight before his 30th birthday.

Born Mark Feld and raised in post-war Stoke Newington, Mark grew up listening to American rock and roll. His parents encouraged his early musical interests; they bought him his first guitar and at the age of 13 Mark saw his idol Eddie Cochran perform one of his last concerts at the Hackney Empire, where it said that the young fan was allowed to carry Cochran's guitar to his waiting car. Cochran was killed in a car crash some days later.

Mark played in skiffle bands and tried his hand at modelling, but in 1965 he secured a record deal, changed his name to Marc Bolan and released his first single 'The Wizard'. After some moderate success he went on to form the rock group 'Tyrannosaurus Rex' and the first singles 'Debora' and 'One Inch Rock' began to creep into the top 40; but still stardom was proving to be evasive. In 1970 Bolan played the very first Pilton Pop, Folk & Blues Festival, a small hippy gathering near Glastonbury that would go on to become the world's leading music festival.

Later that year Bolan contracted the band's name to T Rex, and left the folk roots behind to embrace a more electric psychedelic sound. The first single 'Ride a White Swan' peaked at number 2 in the charts. Bolan took to wearing glitter make-up and colourful satin outfits with a feather boa and top hat, pioneering the glam rock fashions that were to typify the early seventies. T Rex topped the charts in 1971 with their next single 'Hot Love' and over the next two years there followed a succession of genre-defining hits, including 'Get It On', 'Metal Guru', 'Children of the Revolution' and '20th Century Boy'.

By the mid-seventies T Rex's enormous success was beginning to fade as Bolan attempted to expand and experiment with the band's sound; they continued to record albums and release singles but Bolan was also battling drug and alcohol dependency as well as a preoccupation with breaking the American market. In 1975 Bolan and girlfriend, the American singer Gloria Jones, welcomed a son. Bolan cleaned himself up and began to record a pop music TV series called 'Marc' which attracted viewing figures in excess of 10 million every week.

On 16 September 1977 Bolan and Jones were returning home from a Mayfair club in their Mini when Jones lost control of the car on a bridge in southwest London. Bolan was killed instantly when the car hit a tree. The crash site and 'Bolan Tree' in Barnes have become a shrine and place of pilgrimage for fans; on the 25th anniversary of his death a memorial stone with bronze bust was erected. An action group made up of fans was granted a lease of ownership to care for the site.

Bolan's funeral took place at Golders Green Crematorium and was attended by hundreds of fans as well as his friends David Bowie and Rod Stewart. His ashes were interred in a rose bed in the grounds. Two memorial plaques are situated in the west memorial court, alongside that of The Who drummer Keith Moon.

HALFWAY TO PARADISE

BILLY FURY (d 1983)

As Billy Fury, Ronald Wycherley found fame as one of the greatest, but largely forgotten, stars in the history of British pop music; he paved the way for his fellow city folk, The Beatles, to change the face of music forever.

The young Ron worked in the Liverpool Docks with ambitions of stardom. Heavily influenced by the new Country & Western and Rock & Roll records crossing the Atlantic, Ron started his own skiffle band called the 'Formby Sniffle Group', named after the tugboat on which he worked.

In an effort to help her son's fledgling career, Ron's mother wrote to the great London musical impresario of the time, Larry Parnes. Parnes was touring with Marty Wilde in October 1958 and arranged to see the young hopeful when he passed through Liverpool.

Following a brief audition Parnes had seen enough and decided to put Ron on the stage that very night to great acclaim. In a historic yet improbable turn of events, Parnes signed him up immediately and, in keeping with the fashion at the time, gave him a stage name. Billy Fury joined the tour and made his professional debut the following night in Manchester.

Fury's first single 'Maybe Tomorrow' was released in 1959, reaching number 18 in the charts. There followed a glittering pop career with 23 consecutive top 40 singles, including 'Halfway To Paradise' which remained in the UK charts for nearly six months. Although he enjoyed prolonged and continuous success, Fury never made it to No.1. His self-penned debut album *The Sound Of Fury* didn't enjoy immediate acclaim either, but it is now considered one of the greatest early British Rock & Roll albums.

There were many hopefuls to audition as Fury's backing group, one of those that nearly made the grade were a new Liverpool band called the Silver Beetles. The job was offered at £20 per week on the condition that the band sacked their bass player Stuart Sutcliffe, his band mate John Lennon refused, but only after he had got Fury's autograph. The job finally went to The Tornados. The Beatles, on the other hand, continued to play their legendary lunchtime slots at the Cavern Club and were soon to eclipse the sound of Fury. The new Merseybeat sound which developed from skiffle and early Rock & Roll spawned hundreds of new groups vying for prominence, but only one broke through like no other. Fury suddenly found that the competition was fierce and his last top 40 hit came in the frenzied wake of Beatlemania in 1966.

Fury's star began to fade due to ill health. With his continuous heart problems and lifelong battle with rheumatic fever he couldn't maintain his touring schedule and was forced to take long breaks between projects. After a series of heart operations Fury came out of his enforced retirement in the early eighties, but only briefly. His last public appearance came late in 1982; two months later he had died at the age of 42. His well-maintained plot at Mill Hill Cemetery remains a popular destination for dedicated fans.

THE SPY WHO KNEW TOO MUCH

ALEXANDER LITVINENKO (d 2006)

In November 2006 the Russian dissident Alexander Litvinenko made news headlines around the world after he was poisoned with an apparently lethal dose of a radioactive isotope at a London hotel. Three weeks later Litvinenko died at University College Hospital of heart failure resulting from radiation poisoning, he was found to have ingested five times the lethal dose of the highly-toxic polonium-210.

Prior to his slow, painful and public assassination, Litvinenko had been a vocal critic of his former government and in particular President Vladimir Putin. He'd served as an officer for the Russian Federal Security Service (FSB), the agency that replaced the KGB following the collapse of the Soviet Union, but after investigating the attempted murder of Russian tycoon Boris Berezovsky in 1998 he ended up accusing his superiors of ordering the assassination themselves. Litvinenko was arrested but fled with his family to the UK where he was granted asylum.

Whilst in exile Litvinenko took up a consulting position with the British Intelligence Services and from the apparent safety of the UK he also undertook an immensely critical and high profile campaign against the Putin administration, outlining a series of accusations and conspiracy theories in his book *Blowing Up Russia: Terror from Within*.

The murder of an intelligence agent in itself would not have caused such great alarm but when it concerns a deadly radioactive material that was brought into the country with the express intention of being used to kill a naturalised British citizen the authorities tend to take more of an interest. In arranging the murder of one man, Litvinenko's killers are thought to have exposed tens of thousands of people to the potentially lethal effects of radiation.

Police investigating the polonium trail at various locations around London found that very high levels of radioactivity were recorded at the Millennium Hotel in Mayfair's Grosvenor Square, just across the road from the US Embassy, which is where they believe Litvinenko's cup of tea was poisoned during a meeting with former KGB contacts. His was the first ever recorded death from polonium-210 induced radiation poisoning. At least 140 people in London were also confirmed to have been contaminated, which included hotel staff and guests as well as hospital staff, relatives and friends. The long-term health risks remain uncertain.

Following a Scotland Yard investigation in 2007 the Chief Prosecutor suggested that Litvinenko's murder was a government sanctioned execution and British authorities have sought the extradition of their prime suspect from Russia to face charges in the UK, but so far all attempts have been rejected. The Litvinenko affair has led to an intense cooling of diplomatic relations between the two countries. The British counter-intelligence services (MI5) have suggested that the levels of Russian spy activity in the United Kingdom over recent years are comparable with those during the Cold War.

Litvinenko converted to Islam on his deathbed and so prior to his funeral a memorial service was held at Regent's Park Mosque, although Muslim funeral rites could not be carried out for fear of contamination.

He was buried at Highgate's West Cemetery in a lead-lined and sealed coffin in an effort to minimise the effect of radioactive pollution in the ground. Initially his family had wanted to have him cremated but, although Polonium has a relatively short half-life of just 138 days, they were told that they would have to wait for more than 20 years for the radioactivity to reach safe levels. The touching epitaph, dedicated by his widow Marina, reads, 'To the world you are one person but to one person you are the world.'

PUNK PROVOCATUER
MALCOLM McLAREN (d 2010)

Malcolm McLaren has been described as many things, and not all of them complimentary, but he is chiefly remembered as the self-aggrandising architect of 'Punk Rock' and as the manager of The Sex Pistols.

McLaren left art college and with his girlfriend Vivienne Westwood they opened a Teddy boy themed clothing shop called 'Let It Rock' on Chelsea's Kings Road, which they rebranded at a later stage as a fetish wear shop called 'SEX'. In 1975 McLaren worked for a while with glam-punk group the New York Dolls and, inspired by the emerging US punk scene he returned to London with the idea of forming his own band. He brought together aspiring musicians and SEX customers Steve Jones, Paul Cook and Glen Matlock, and introduced them to a green haired Johnny Rotten who auditioned to an Alice Cooper record and clearly couldn't sing, but McLaren liked his attitude and was convinced he would make the perfect front man.

The Sex Pistols' first two singles, 'Anarchy in the U.K.' and the controversial 'God Save the Queen' which was released at the time of the Queen's Silver Jubilee, in 1977, and subsequently banned by the BBC, served as a rallying cry to the disenfranchised youth of depressed seventies Britain. Social misfits and outcasts came together under an umbrella of rebellion, arcane fashion and discordant garage rock. The Sex Pistols found themselves at the epicentre of a new youth movement; they were the embodiment of Punk and McLaren its self-styled impresario.

McLaren excelled at marketing and publicity, he was the master of the cheap gimmick and would consistently guarantee column inches for both the band and himself, but even he could not have reckoned with the sheer outrage that the Sex Pistols created in the media following their appearance on the *Today* programme with host Bill Grundy who goaded the band into swearing on live TV. Their star burned brightly for just three years and one album before McLaren was accused of mismanagement and the band eventually split up. Their influence on alternative music and youth culture were far greater than anyone could have predicted. McLaren went on to manage other acts before embarking on a solo music career with hits such as 'Buffalo Gals' and 'Double Dutch', but eventually the Sex Pistols took McLaren to court for unpaid royalties and the relationship soured considerably from there, he and Rotten never spoke again.

In 2009 McLaren was diagnosed with mesothelioma, a rare and untreatable abdominal cancer, and passed away at a Swiss clinic six months later. He was given a characteristically colourful send-off; his coffin was emblazoned with the slogan 'Too fast to live, too young to die' and his funeral service, held at a deconsecrated Church in Marylebone, was attended by his former partner Dame Vivienne Westwood, artist Tracey Emin, Sex Pistols band members Cook and Matlock and musicians Adam Ant and Sir Bob Geldof.

There followed a procession through north London to Highgate cemetery for his interment. The horse-drawn carriage was decorated with typically 'punk' floral tributes, which included the 'Anarchy' symbol and the motto 'Cash from Chaos'. Mourners followed in a double decker bus as a sound system blasted out punk classics, including the Sid Vicious version of Sinatra's 'My Way'. Well-wishers gathered en-route and brought the streets to a standstill in Camden Town as fans, punks and confused shoppers lined the street for a 'minute of mayhem' to say their last goodbye as the cortege passed.

McLaren's black granite headstone, installed in April 2013, features a bronze death mask created by the sculptor Nick Reynolds, son of the man who masterminded the Great Train Robbery, Bruce Reynolds. His fitting epitaph reads, 'Better a spectacular failure, than a benign success.'

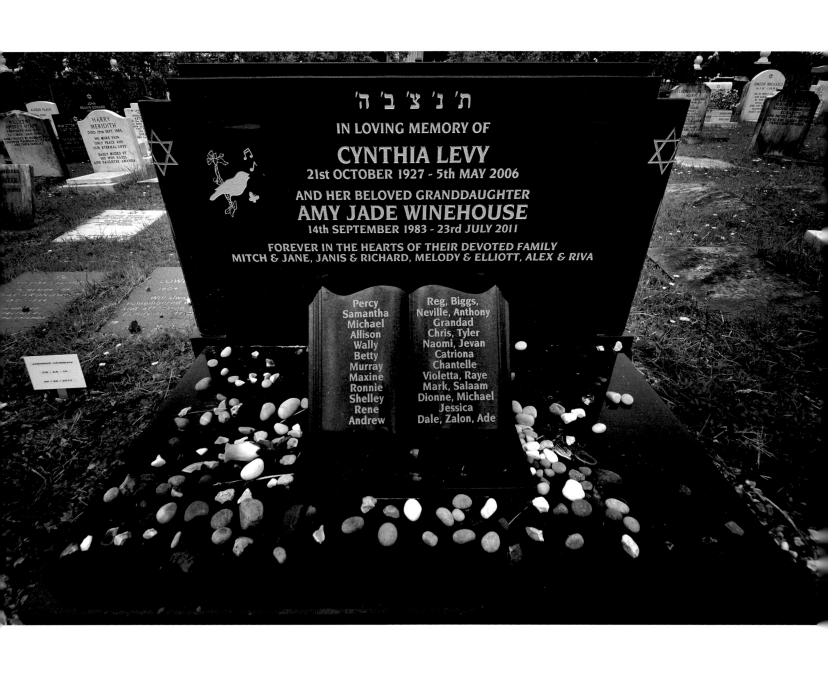

BACK TO BLACK
AMY WINEHOUSE (d 2011)

Amidst the peaceful and secluded surroundings of Edgwarebury Jewish Cemetery, where the suburbia of North London meets rolling fields, there lies the final resting place of one of the most outstanding talents of her generation.

In her short but eventful career Amy Winehouse released just two albums, *Frank* in 2003, and *Back to Black* in 2006 for which she won an unprecedented five Grammy awards; her effortless, soulful voice brought her instant global success. In 2004 Winehouse won an Ivor Novello Award for her debut single 'Stronger Than Me' and *Frank* was also nominated for the Mercury Prize.

The following year, after separating from her boyfriend Blake Fielder-Civil, Winehouse was inspired to pour her heartbreak into writing her critically acclaimed second album. During this time she began to display her rebellious nature by overindulging in drugs and alcohol, which would see her in and out of rehab for years to come, whilst also acquiring the tattoos for which she would become famous.

In 2007 Winehouse entered into a brief but turbulent marriage with Fielder-Civil and she became absorbed into a self-destructive cycle of drug addiction. The tragic soap opera of her life became regular tabloid fodder and every misdemeanour, including assault charges in 2009, was reported by the media around the world. The infamy of her drug abuse had overtaken the artistry of her music.

Her family and fans alike had always feared for her health and in July 2011 those fears were finally realised when she was found dead at her home in Camden. Speculation was rife as to the cause but an inquest recorded a verdict of accidental alcohol poisoning; she had drunk herself to death. Her music had touched many millions of fans and the outpouring of grief was palpable, crowds gathered in vigil outside her home in Camden Square and it still continues to attract the hordes in solemn pilgrimage.

The death of Winehouse brought further credence to the cultural phenomenon known as the '27 Club', a growing band of notable musicians who, at the very peak of their careers all lost their lives prematurely at the same age. She joins the likes of Jimi Hendrix, Kurt Cobain, Brian Jones, Janis Joplin and Jim Morrison. Although the age of 27 is entirely coincidental, it is telling how the twin demons of drug and alcohol dependence are often the price paid for genius and fame.

A private funeral service was carried out at Edgwarebury Cemetery before her cremation at Golders Green Crematorium where the eyes of the world's media looked on. Her ashes were interred with those of her grandmother, Cynthia, whose name she'd had tattooed on her arm. In September 2012 a black marble headstone was erected, inscribed with pink lettering. It features a singing bird that replicates another tattoo Winehouse wore on her right forearm. A raised ledger lists the names of family members, but also those of notable friends and colleagues, such as her goddaughter, singer Dionne Bromfield, producer Mark Ronson, manager Raye Cosbert and her boyfriend Reg Traviss. The name of her former husband is notable by its absence.

Following her death *Back to Black* went on to become the UK's highest-selling album of the 21st century and has sold more than 20 million copies worldwide.

On what would have been the singer's 28th birthday the Winehouse family launched 'The Amy Winehouse Foundation' to help young people to overcome drug and alcohol addiction.

West Norwood Cemetery

SOUTH
LONDON

THE CUP THAT CHEERS

THOMAS TWINING (d 1741)

Tea had been drunk in China for thousands of years before it came to these shores in the mid 17th century. Already popular amongst the European aristocracy, it wasn't until 1660, when King Charles II returned from exile, that tea became fashionable. The King's new wife, Catherine de Braganza, a Portuguese princess, was an avid tea drinker and her influence in court created a sensation in London society. However, tea was still a rare commodity and a prohibitive import tax meant it could only be afforded by the wealthy. This began to change when the powerful East India Company, who had long established trade routes based on cotton and silk, began to import tea from Canton.

Tea gradually found its way into London's numerous coffee shops. These bawdy and rough establishments each catered to a specific clientele; merchants would meet for business in one, whilst poets might while away their days in another. All walks of city life gathered to eat and drink together. But this was a world exclusively inhabited by men, as ladies of reputation dared not enter.

That was until the pioneering businessman Thomas Twining, an apprentice of the East India Company, saw a gap in the market and introduced the first teashop, 'Tom's', in 1706. He chose his site well, amidst the high society of Westminster. His menu offered fine dry teas as well as coffees, but more importantly it was an establishment that welcomed women of all classes.

Twining's popularity and reputation as a purveyor of quality teas quickly grew.

Twining's empire expanded, his son Daniel began to export tea to the Americas and his grandson, Richard, negotiated a cut in tea duties with the Prime Minister, William Pitt, making tea affordable to all. In 1787 Richard Twining re-branded his grandfather's business with the same typeface that appears on Twining's products today. At more than two centuries it is considered the oldest corporate logo in use in the world.

During the 18th century tea became a traditional fixture in everyday home life. The quality of London's water was so poor that ale had been widely drunk as the common accompaniment to breakfast, but tea gradually established itself as the alternative. Dingy coffee houses gave way to the more sophisticated tea gardens and from here the complex social rituals associated with afternoon tea developed.

The year Queen Victoria came to the throne she granted Twinings a Royal Warrant for tea and this has continued for every successive British monarch. Tea had fixed itself in the culture and consciousness of the British people; we had become a nation of tea drinkers and Thomas Twining's dynasty was largely to thank for playing such a significant part.

Twining's memorial tablet, on the north-east corner of St Mary Twickenham, overlooks neighbouring Dial House, the home he built in the 1720s.

HEAVENS ABOVE

EDMOND HALLEY (d 1742)

In 1675 King Charles II founded the Royal Observatory at Greenwich and instructed his first Astronomer Royal, John Flamsteed, to chart the skies of the Northern hemisphere to aid navigation at sea, whilst a young Edmond Halley, fresh from University, journeyed to the British territory of Saint Helena in the South Atlantic to chart the fixed stars of the southern hemisphere.

Halley made many accurate astronomical observations, which included the first transit of Mercury, but it is for his work on comets that he has become best known; the most famous comet of all is undoubtedly the one named after him, Halley's Comet.

Sightings of the comet had been made over thousands of years by ancient Greek and Chinese astronomers, even making an appearance on the Bayeux Tapestry as an omen of Harold II's defeat at the Battle of Hastings in 1066, but it was Halley who first put forward the theory that the comet was periodic.

Halley made calculations, based on Newton's new laws of physics, from historical records of comet sightings and concluded that they were in fact the same comet returning on its orbit of the sun. Halley predicted that the comet was due to return to Earth in 1758. He was proved correct but did not live to see the realisation of his theory. He achieved lasting fame when the comet was named in his honour in 1759. Halley's Comet last appeared in 1986 and is predicted to next appear in 2061. He carried out extensive meteorological and atmospheric observations and made studies into the Earth's magnetic fields, eclipses and polar aurora.

Halley also invented an early form of diving bell and a liquid compass for use on ships, and he also made the first attempt to date the monument at Stonehenge using scientific methods, but it was his overriding interest in physics that led him to publish Isaac Newton's great masterpiece the *Principia,* in which Newton detailed the laws of gravity and motion. Halley later succeeded Flamsteed as Astronomer Royal in 1720, a position he held until his death in 1742.

Halley was buried in what is now the Old Churchyard at St Margaret's in Lee, about a mile from the Royal Observatory at Greenwich. The original cover to Halley's chest tomb was removed to the Royal Observatory for preservation; the Latin inscription reads, 'Under this marble peacefully rests, with his beloved wife, Edmond Halley, LL.D. unquestionably the greatest astronomer of his age. As when living he was so highly esteemed by his countrymen, gratitude requires that his memory should be respected by posterity.' In 1836 the sixth Astronomer Royal John Pond was buried with Halley in the same tomb. Nearby there is also the grave of the fourth Astronomer Royal Nathaniel Bliss.

PRIME TARGET

SPENCER PERCEVAL (d 1812)

Spencer Perceval holds the rather inglorious distinction of being the only British Prime Minister to have been assassinated in office.

After serving as leader of the House of Commons and Chancellor of the Exchequer, Perceval took office in 1809 following the death of his predecessor the Duke of Portland. As a Tory Prime Minister in the early 19th century Perceval presided over a tumultuous period in British history, and not only that but he had to do it with precious little backing; he had only one other member in his cabinet, and he even had to act as his own Chancellor.

Britain was at war with the French; Napoleon's forces were engaged by the Duke of Wellington during the Peninsula War in Spain. The Napoleonic Wars had put a great strain on the country's finances and Britain was in severe economic depression.

The burgeoning Industrial Revolution had brought about great social upheaval and created harsh working conditions in factories, which in turn led to the Luddite rebellion. As if this wasn't enough of a burden, Perceval had to also deal with the delicate matters of state surrounding the worsening mental illness of King George III and the establishment of the Regency.

But, it would seem that Perceval was more than sufficient to the task; he started to receive increasing support as he maintained stability and the situation began to improve. However on the evening of 11 May 1812, just two years and 221 days into Perceval's administration, an assailant calmly stepped forward and shot the Prime Minister through the heart in the lobby of the House of Commons. Perceval maintained a faint pulse, but was declared dead a short while later.

Initially it was thought that the attacker, John Bellingham, was a member of a Luddite terrorist plot, but it transpired that he had acted alone. He had been wrongly imprisoned in Russia whilst on business and petitioned the government for compensation on his return, but without success. He took his grievance to the Foreign Office where he was brushed aside and told to take whatever measures he thought necessary. So Bellingham bought two .50 calibre pistols, tailored secret pockets into his coat and made his way to the House of Commons where he carried out his revenge. He put up no resistance and was tried and hanged the day before Perceval's funeral.

Perceval left a widow, six sons and six daughters, aged between three and twenty. He had only £100 in the bank at the time of his death, so Parliament voted in favour of settling a sum of £50,000 for the benefit of his twelve children.

He was buried in a vault at St Luke's Church, Charlton, during a private funeral. Among the pall-bearers were the Lord Chancellor, Home Secretary and Perceval's successor, the Earl of Liverpool. A memorial showing a relief of the assassination was unveiled in the nave of Westminster Abbey by the Prince Regent in 1822 'to mark the nation's abhorrence of the act by which he fell'.

NEAR THIS PLACE ARE THE MORTAL REMAINS OF
THE RIGHT HONORABLE SPENCER PERCEVAL.
FIRST LORD OF THE TREASURY.
AND CHANCELLOR OF THE EXCHEQUER.
WHO DIED ON THE 11TH OF MAY A.D. 1812.
IN THE COMMONS HOUSE OF PARLIAMENT.
IN THE 50TH YEAR OF HIS AGE.
HIS NOBLEST EPITAPH IS THE REGRET OF
HIS SOVEREIGN AND HIS COUNTRY.
HIS MOST SPLENDID MONUMENT THE GLORY OF ENGLAND.
BY HIS COUNSELS MAINTAINED, EXALTED, AMPLIFIED,
BUT THE HAND OF THE ASSASSIN
NOT ONLY BROKE ASUNDER THE BRILLIANT CHAINS OF DUTY
WHICH BIND THE STATESMAN TO HIS NATIVE LAND.
AND MADE A VOID IN THE HIGH
AND ELOQUENT COUNCILS OF THE NATION:
IT SEVERED TIES MORE TENDER AND DELICATE.
THOSE OF CONJUGAL AND PARENTAL AFFECTION.
AND TURNED A HOME OF PEACE AND LOVE, INTO A HOUSE OF
MOURNING AND DESOLATION.

SACRED
TO THE MEMORY OF
WILLIAM BLIGH ESQUIRE F.R.S.
VICE ADMIRAL OF THE BLUE.
THE CELEBRATED NAVIGATOR
WHO FIRST TRANSPLANTED THE BREAD FRUIT TREE
FROM OTAHEITE TO THE WEST INDIES
BRAVELY FOUGHT THE BATTLES OF HIS COUNTRY
AND DIED BELOVED, RESPECTED, AND LAMENTED
ON THE 7 DAY OF DECEMBER 1817.
AGED 64.

MUTINY ON THE HIGH SEAS

WILLIAM BLIGH (d 1817)

History has not been kind to William Bligh. As Lieutenant of *HMS Bounty* Bligh will forever be remembered as a tyrannical sea commander who drove his crew to mutiny; but it is difficult to distinguish historic fact from embellished fiction. At a time in the late 18th century when the Royal Navy press-ganged many of its crews into unwilling service, mutinies were not uncommon, but what made the *Bounty* such a prominent case was Bligh's heroism in the face of desperate odds and not the perceived ruthlessness of his leadership.

On 23 December 1787 Lieutenant Bligh set sail bound for the South Pacific island of Otaheite (Tahiti), where he would collect a consignment of Breadfruit plants and transport them to the slave plantations of the colonial West Indies as a high-energy food crop. Bligh was put in command of a ragged crew, and as the only commissioned officer on board he appointed his good friend and companion of previous voyages, Fletcher Christian, as Master's Mate.

It took them a perilous ten months to reach Tahiti, and they spent a further six months growing the Breadfruit saplings in preparation for their journey back. But when the time came his men were reluctant to leave behind the tropical climate and welcoming local women; Bligh's prolonged shore leave in paradise had inadvertently sewn the seeds of rebellion.

Tensions were running high when, three weeks into the return journey, Bligh accused Christian of theft after some coconuts had gone missing; it was this trivial matter that led a demoralised crew to mutiny. Christian took control of the ship and cast Bligh adrift in a cramped longboat with eighteen loyal crew members and meagre provisions. In what is considered one of the most epic feats of naval navigation in history, Bligh fought the elements and starvation to bring his men back alive. They travelled a staggering 3600 miles in 42 days, to make landfall on the island of Timor. Christian and his mutineers retuned to their lives in Tahiti, but then to evade capture they travelled a further 2000 miles and settled on the uninhabited Pitcairn Island, where they set fire to *The Bounty*. Their idyll was short lived however as infighting with their Tahitian settlers led to Christian's death.

The accepted misunderstanding of actual events was established in 1932 with the publication of the fictionalised *Bounty Trilogy* of historic novels. Subsequent Hollywood screen adaptations then portrayed Fletcher Christian as the handsome swashbuckling hero, played by the likes of Errol Flynn, Clark Gable and Marlon Brando, opposite the villainous and sadistic Bligh as his brooding nemesis.

Although his fame is almost entirely based upon the fate of *HMS Bounty*, Bligh is also remembered as a well-respected naturalist. He travelled extensively and provided many new plant specimens to the Royal Botanical Gardens at Kew. The scientific genus for the Jamaican fruit tree 'Ackee' is named Blighia in his honour.

William Bligh led a distinguished and colourful 44-year career. During a time in which the British Navy ruled the waves Bligh had been fortunate enough to serve with both Captain Cook and Admiral Nelson. Although he remained a controversial figure to the end, he was promoted through the Royal Navy colours, eventually succeeding to Vice Admiral of the Blue in 1814.

He was buried with his wife, beneath a splendid tomb of Coade stone, in the graveyard of St Mary at Lambeth, alongside the pioneering botanists and gardeners John Tradescant, the elder and younger. In keeping with the horticultural tradition of its distinguished residents, the church has become a museum to gardening history.

NINETEENTH CENTURY NIGELLA

ISABELLA BEETON (d 1865)

Isabella Mary Mayson Beeton is known the world over as the original 'domestic goddess' and precursor to the celebrity chef. When she published her seminal, bestselling *Book of Household Management* in 1861, she popularised the concept of the cookbook and shaped the future for the likes of Delia Smith, Gordon Ramsay and the multitude of TV chefs we are presented with today.

Mrs Beeton was inspired to write her historic opus because she judged that 'there is no more fruitful source of family discontent than a housewife's badly-cooked dinners and untidy ways'. She wrote regular articles for the *Englishwoman's Domestic Magazine,* which was published by her husband Samuel Beeton. The magazine was ground-breaking in being the first of its kind aimed specifically at women. Together they published the full collection of 2751 entries as a book, to critical acclaim, selling more than 60,000 copies in its first year.

The book offered a wealth of recipes and cooking advice, covering everything from 'Calf's Head Soup' to 'Lobster Curry', 'Aunt Nelly's Treacle Pudding' and 'Lemonade for Invalids', even estimating the time and financial cost for every dish. Likening the enterprise of home management to that of an army commander, she wrote about the fascinating details of life with extraordinary candour, providing a charming insight into all aspects of polite Victorian society. On choosing one's friends she recommends, 'a gossiping acquaintance, who indulges in the scandal and ridicule of her neighbours, should be avoided as a pestilence' and on completing a dinner party 'the French have a habit of gargling the mouth; but it is a custom which no English gentlewoman should, in the slightest degree, imitate'.

To have compiled such a significant collection of works it is often assumed that Mrs Beeton was the archetypal old maid, when in fact she began to write at the age of 21 and was a thoroughly modern woman for her time. She contracted septicaemia and died a week after the birth of her fourth child at the age of 28. In a twist of further misfortune Samuel was forced to sell the copyright to the *Book of Household Management*, as well as a whole host of titles he had published under the Beeton name, when the Overend & Gurney bank collapsed just a year after his wife's death, leaving him close to bankruptcy.

The Beeton grave is marked by a plain headstone in West Norwood Cemetery, which was erected in 1933 after the original had fallen into decay.

ARABIAN KNIGHT

SIR RICHARD FRANCIS BURTON (d 1890)

The rich tapestry of British endeavour is peppered with a multitude of eccentric characters, but few are quite so colourful and fascinating as the controversial Victorian adventurer, writer, orientalist, diplomat and accomplished linguist, Richard Francis Burton.

Whilst serving with the army of the East India Company in Bombay, Burton made a name for himself by studying the culture, participating in the customs and learning the dialects of the local people. It is said that in his lifetime he had mastered somewhere in the region of forty languages and dialects. He was such a skilled linguist that he could often travel in disguise, not only fooling the locals but also his fellow officers who knew him well.

Burton was thirsty for adventure and sought funding to carry out an expedition to the Holy City of Mecca disguised as a Muslim pilgrim. If his true identity as a non-Muslim European were discovered the penalty would have been death. His preparations were so meticulous that he even underwent circumcision in keeping with Muslim tradition. Burton succeeded in his pilgrimage, safely returning to write what became an immensely popular three-volume book.

His next sponsored expedition was into Africa to explore the country of Somalia, but his party came under attack and Burton was speared through the face, penetrating both cheeks, leaving him with deep facial scarring. Undeterred, he began another expedition to find the source of the Nile and explore the great lakes of the African interior, becoming the first westerner to find Lake Tanganyika.

Burton travelled extensively and wrote prolifically. He entered the Foreign Service in 1861 and was appointed British Consul to the Equatorial Guinea island of Fernando Po, later to take posts in Brazil and Syria. Whilst stationed in Trieste he began to write and publish the controversial literature for which he is best known. He wrote a translation of the Hindu *Kama Sutra* in 1883, followed by a sexualised translation of the Islamic *Arabian Nights* stories, and also *The Perfumed Garden* a fifteenth-century work of erotic Arabic literature. The chattering classes of polite Victorian society were horrified by Burton's scandalous books and the only way he could avoid prosecution for obscenity was to print his 'pornographic' manuscripts privately for subscribers only.

Following Burton's death in Trieste his wife Isabel burned many of his papers and wrote a biography of her husband dedicated 'To my earthly master, who is waiting for me on heaven's frontiers'. Burton's mausoleum, in the churchyard of St Mary Magdalen Catholic Church in Mortlake, was built at his request in the form of a Bedouin desert tent so that he and Isabel may lie beside each other for eternity. A poem of dedication begins 'Farewell Dead Hero, The great life is ended, the great perils, the great joys; and he to whom adventures were as toys.'

The exterior sandstone walls were carved to represent the ripples of tent canvas hanging over supporting ropes and are decorated with an Ottoman star and crescent motif. Visitors are invited to climb a ladder at the rear where a purpose built window reveals the two caskets, Isabel's mahogany coffin on the left and Burton's steel sarcophagus on the right. A mirror situated on the far wall allows the viewer to see the details of a small marble altar and tabernacle beneath the window. From the ceiling there hang lamps and a series of camel bells which play a chime on entering. Interior embellishments also include glass flasks, which are said to contain water collected from Mecca's sacred well, and devotional paintings hanging above each coffin.

The fabric of the tomb has suffered neglect and vandalism over the years but it has now undergone extensive cleaning and a sympathetic restoration. It is a fitting tribute to such a unique individual that he is memorialised in such a singular manner.

BREATH OF FRESH AIR

SIR JOSEPH BAZALGETTE (d 1891)

As a consequence of London's rapid expansion in the 18th and 19th centuries, the city, and especially the River Thames, began to resemble something of an open sewer. Fish could not survive in the river and Londoners were dying in their thousands from cholera.

London had never been a particularly sanitary city. The antiquated sewerage system that was in place was only designed for rainwater, and it was certainly failing to cope with the demands of an increasing population. To make matters worse, a new design of flushing toilet had been introduced across the city and the additional waste water began to flood the thousands of cesspits that were used to collect human waste. This culminated in 'The Great Stink', a public health crisis that occurred during the particularly hot summer of 1858. The entire city was overflowing with effluent and the stench was overwhelming. It got so bad the Government even considered evacuating parliament to a safe distance from the city.

They were desperate times and short term measures were not going to solve the crisis. In response, the Government appointed a Metropolitan Board of Works to build the infrastructure that would cope with a population in excess of two million. Joseph Bazalgette was elected as chief engineer.

Bazalgette had been previously employed with the expansion of the railway network, but now he was tasked with designing and building a modern sewerage system that would transform the city. By installing an extensive 82-mile network of intercepting sewers north and south of the river, fed by thousands of miles of local sewers, Bazalgette's system avoided the Thames altogether. Waste was pumped towards east London where it would be released into the tidal estuary and out to sea. By the time the system was fully operational in 1874 the population had doubled to four million. Bazalgette had luckily overestimated the dimensions of his sewers and the network was more than capable of coping with the extra demand. By removing sewage from the daily lives of Londoners, Bazalgette had also brought an end to the epidemics of cholera and typhoid that had ravaged the population.

London's continued growth has put pressure on the capacity of the Victorian sewers but Bazalgette's network still forms the backbone of the city's current system and it is rightly placed amongst the seven wonders of the industrial world, alongside the likes of the Panama Canal and the Hoover Dam.

The impact Bazalgette had on London is immeasurable and he was knighted for his achievements by Queen Victoria in 1875. In 2011 his great-great-grandson, television producer Peter Bazalgette, was also knighted, but his achievements are far less impressive, he developed the reality television show *Big Brother*.

Joseph Bazalgette lived and died in Wimbledon and in keeping with the scale of his engineering success his monumental, Grade II listed, subterranean mausoleum dominates the churchyard of St Mary's.

IN LOVING MEMORY OF
SIR HENRY TATE, BARONET.
BORN 11TH MARCH
DIED 5TH DECEMBER 189

"HE HATH DISPERS
TO THE POOR; HIS RIGHTEOU
NDURETH FOR EVER" PSALM CXII.

ALSO
AMY,
SIR HENRY TATE, BARONET.
11TH JANUARY 1850,
DIED 18TH OCTOBER

SUGAR DADDY
SIR HENRY TATE (d 1899)

The name Tate is synonymous with art and sugar, and it was the philanthropic tycoon Sir Henry Tate who brought both to the British populace.

The son of a Lancashire clergyman, the young Henry was apprenticed as a humble grocer but he excelled in business and had expanded to a chain of six stores across Liverpool by his mid-thirties, but it was with sugar that he'd make his fortune.

Tate became a partner in a sugar refinery in 1859 and within ten years he had bought the business outright, naming it Henry Tate & Sons. Tate was always trying to innovate the refining process to make his sugar purer, but more significantly he bought the licence to a German patent for the method of producing cubed sugar. Tate recognised that this simple process would make easily portioned sugar ideal for domestic use. His Thames refinery was opened to specialise in the production of sugar cubes and the business grew rapidly. It was in 1921 that Tate's company merged with rivals Abram Lyle & Sons, best known for their Golden Syrup, to form the familiar Tate & Lyle brand that we recognise today.

It isn't so much his great wealth that Henry Tate is remembered for, but the benevolence with which he shared it. It was said to be his rule that he would give half of his income to the good of the public. He made generous donations to charities, colleges and hospitals; founding the university library at Liverpool with £42,000, as well as making provision for free libraries in Streatham, Lambeth and Brixton.

Tate became a great patron of the arts and collected many paintings by leading contemporary British artists, such as Sir Edwin Landseer and the Pre-Raphaelites Millais and Waterhouse. He proudly displayed them in a purpose-built gallery at his home Park Hill, in south London, to which he allowed the public access on Sundays; the very first Tate gallery.

In the 1890s the government declared that there was insufficient British art in the National Gallery and Tate pledged his collection for the gratification of the nation. Unfortunately there was not the space to accommodate his gift and the offer was turned down.

Tate did not give up though and commenced the building of his own gallery, in 1895, on the bank of the Thames at a cost of nearly half a million pounds. The Prince of Wales opened the National Gallery of British Art, later becoming known as Tate Britain, in 1897.

Tate was made a baronet in 1898. Being a modest man he had declined the honour on two previous occasions, but was told that a third refusal would be an insult to the Royal family. He died the following year and was buried at West Norwood cemetery. His impressive red terracotta mausoleum, which was designed by Sidney Smith the architect of Tate's gallery, is now a Grade II listed building. His epitaph, from *Psalms*, reads, 'he hath dispersed, he hath given to the poor, his righteousness endureth for ever.'

Today the Tate operates across four sites, at Tate's Britain, Modern, Liverpool and St Ives, providing free public access to its British, international, modern and contemporary art collections, attracting more than 7 million visitors a year; a fitting legacy to a greatly generous man.

NEWS OF THE WORLD
BARON PAUL JULIUS DE REUTER (d 1899)

The 21st century has brought significant advances in communications technology and our insatiable appetite for global news is fed by this. It is somewhat abstract therefore to imagine that the history of news gathering began with carrier pigeons.

The pioneering German entrepreneur Israel Beer Josaphat changed his name to Paul Julius Reuter when he married and converted to Christianity. Reuter moved to Paris to work as a translator for Charles-Louis Havas, who founded the news agency AFP (Agence France-Presse). But his interest in politics and business, coupled with his familiarity with early telegraphy, led him to set up his own financial news service in Aachen, on the German/Belgian border.

In 1849 Reuter began running stock price dispatches between Paris and Berlin, his fleet of pigeons proved to be far quicker than traditional transport methods, and he soon acquired notoriety for the speed of his reports. He would communicate his news to clients via telegraph, thus creating the first Reuters news-wire. As telegraph cable lines were laid across Europe Reuter's service began to expand rapidly.

When the first fully functioning international cable line was laid across the English Channel in 1851, linking Dover to Calais, Reuter was quick to capitalise; he moved his business to London and set up in the Royal Exchange, communicating stock information to the markets of Europe. By 1858 Reuter had started delivering a subscription news service to the British Press, the first of which was sold to the *London Morning Advertiser*. Reuters was the first to report the assassination of Abraham Lincoln in Europe and gained a reputation for 'scooping' the competition.

The first transatlantic cable was laid in 1866 between the west coast of Ireland and Newfoundland, cutting communication times from days to minutes and by the 1870s Reuter had established a full international news service across Europe and the Americas. As the cables further extended to India and the Far East, Reuters became the official news agency to the British Empire, giving it prestige and profitability. By maintaining impartiality and integrity, whilst embracing new technologies, such as satellite communication, the company has remained at the forefront of the news industry ever since.

Reuter took retirement in 1878, passing the business to his son Herbert. He died at his home in the south of France and was buried at the fashionable West Norwood cemetery in a granite pedestal tomb. His inscription provides an ironic footnote to the story, considering Reuter's reputation for accuracy; his middle name is misspelled 'Juluis'.

CRICKETING COLOSSUS

WG GRACE (d 1915)

No one in cricket's long history has made a greater impact or has come to personify the gentleman's game better than the 'old man' WG Grace, the 'father' of modern cricket.

Born William Gilbert Grace in 1848, the fourth of nine children to a cricket obsessed family in Bristol, Grace rose to prominence to become the greatest exponent of the game. In a first class career that spanned 44 years, and totalled more than 54,000 runs, it is astonishing to note that Grace never played professionally.

Grace's interests were primarily in medicine, although it was evident that his true talents lay with cricket. Three years after making his first class debut and already well known as an excellent all-round cricketer, Grace enrolled at Bristol Medical School in 1868. He eventually qualified as a doctor in 1879, at the age of 31, his education much prolonged by his outstanding contributions to Gloucestershire County Cricket Club and the MCC (Marylebone Cricket Club).

Dr Grace first set up practice in Bristol, hiring locums to assist him in the summer months when he played cricket. He travelled between Bristol and London so regularly that it is said trains would wait for him at Paddington station if he had been delayed in the field. Although he played as an amateur, such was his fame that he drew significant rewards from cricket, earning more out of the sport than he did from medicine. He is fondly remembered for treating many of his poorer patients without charge.

In August 1876 Grace made his highest score of 344, for the MCC, it was the first triple century to be recorded in first class cricket. He then went on to make scores of 177 and 318 for Gloucestershire. In three consecutive innings Grace had scored 839 runs. The record for the previous highest score of 278 had stood for 56 years; within a week Grace had beaten it twice. He displayed such considerable skill with the bat that he is said to have developed most of the techniques of modern batting.

Grace made his international test debut against Australia in 1880, alongside his brothers Edward (EM Grace) and Fred (GF Grace), scoring a respectable 152. Having competed in 20 Ashes test matches, Grace bowed out of test cricket when he opened the batting for England at the ripe old age of 50.

Grace is spuriously credited with introducing the practice of sledging, by which players verbally intimidate or distract their opponents. During an exhibition match Grace was caught 'leg before wicket' with the first delivery, the umpire thought better of his decision when Grace famously stood his ground and stated "they have come to watch me bat, not to see you umpire". Another apocryphal tale attributed to Grace suggests that he once hit a ball 36 miles after his shot landed on a passing freight train.

The shadow of the great man still looms large over the game a century on. Throughout his 870-match career Grace revolutionised cricket; such was his draw he single-handedly elevated the game to a major spectator sport and it became a national institution.

His death, at the age of 67 from a heart attack, plunged the nation into deep mourning. At the height of his fame he was the most recognised man in Victorian England. Grace was buried in what remains a well-maintained family plot at Elmers End Cemetery in Beckenham. He was honoured in 1923 with a pair of ornamental memorial gates at Lord's Cricket Ground, dedicated to 'The Great Cricketer'.

HIGH CALIBRE

HIRAM MAXIM (d 1916)

Hiram Maxim was one of the great inventors of the Victorian Age. He conceived an electric light bulb before Thomas Edison and flew an airplane before the Wright Brothers, but he is not credited with either invention. Instead Maxim is chiefly remembered for creating a weapon that was to change the face of modern warfare, the automatic machine gun.

Maxim was born in the United States but after losing a patent dispute with Edison over the filament light bulb he moved to Britain. As the political situation in Europe worsened, an American acquaintance suggested he invent something that would "enable Europeans to cut each other's throats with greater facility". As an instrument of mass murder, no other weapon has killed more people than the machine gun.

Prior to Maxim's gun, machine guns such as the Gatling gun were cumbersome and crank handled. Maxim used the power from the recoil to load the next round and eject the spent cartridge, creating a continuous discharge of over 600 rounds per minute. The British adopted the Maxim gun and first used it in battle in Rhodesia during the First Matabele War of 1893. With just a handful of Maxim guns the troops of the British South Africa Company massacred the Ndebele Zulu warriors in their thousands. Not only was their lethal firepower so devastating, but the psychological advantage over the natives was huge.

The British put the design into production as the Vickers machine gun. Kaiser Wilhelm also showed a keen interest and the German's bought the patent, developing their Maschinengewehr 08, whilst the Russian's built their variation, the Pulemyot Maxim gun. Inevitably, the armies of Europe went to war in 1914 in what was to become the deadliest conflict known to man, resulting in more than 16 million fatalities.

Maxim's ardour didn't stop there; he also played a significant role in the history of early flight. He used much of the vast wealth earned from his gun to conduct some of the earliest experiments into powered flight. Maxim built a flying machine, he called an aeroplane; it was powered by steam, weighed 3.5 tonnes, had a wingspan of 104ft and propellers 18ft in diameter, and in 1894 he achieved flight; Maxim flew his massive and ungainly biplane for 200ft before crashing. It was almost a decade before the Wright brothers are acknowledged as having flown the first 'controlled' and 'sustained' human flight.

Maxim put his flying experience to good use and built one of the earliest innovations in fairground rides. 'Sir Hiram Maxim's Captive Flying Machine' opened in amusement parks across the country in 1904 and the example at Blackpool Pleasure Beach is still in operation to this day, the oldest ride of its kind in Europe. But it wasn't all thrills and spills; Maxim is known too for more everyday inventions such as the mousetrap, curling tongs and an inhaler, which he used for his bronchitis.

He was awarded the Legion d'honneur at the Paris exhibition in 1881 and was knighted by King Edward VII after he succeeded his mother Victoria in 1901. Maxim died in 1916 in the midst of the First World War and is buried at West Norwood Cemetery.

IN MEMORY OF
SIR HIRAM S. MAXIM
1840 ~ 1916.

...AH MAXIM

...~1941.

...UBERT

MAXIM

COL MAXIM

...ARMY 1902~1980

FOOTBALL'S FOUNDING FATHER

EBENEZER COBB MORLEY (d 1924)

In the middle of Barnes Common, hidden amongst the undergrowth, lies the neglected and overgrown Old Cemetery, a quaint two-acre Victorian graveyard that has been left to suffer at the hands of vandals. It is quite a surprise to stumble upon such a sight in the middle of an open public space, but it's even more of a surprise to find, hidden on the periphery, the forgotten grave of the man who founded the Football Association and wrote the rules of modern football.

Ebenezer Cobb Morley was a Yorkshire lawyer who moved to London at the age of 27; he was an enthusiastic sportsman and, having settled in Barnes, he took up rowing. He founded the Barnes and Mortlake Regatta in 1862 and competed at the Henley Regatta in 1864, but it was as the founder and captain of the Barnes Football Club that Morley would make an indelible impact on the sporting world. He proposed that the sport of football should be governed by a single body under a set of unified laws, in a similar way that the MCC administered the sport of cricket.

The early game was first played in mediaeval Britain as 'Mob football', a lawless and riotous gathering of any number of players which often resulted in serious injury and occasionally death, such was the violence involved in attempting to score in the opponent's goal. The game became so out of hand that an attempt was made by King Edward II to ban it. As the game developed it was played for centuries in various forms and with a variety of rules, depending on the school or city being played in. The Cambridge rules, for example, allowed forward passing but prevented running whilst holding the ball, whereas the Sheffield rules introduced the spot kick-off and outlawed the practice of hacking.

In 1863 a meeting of interested parties was convened at the Freemasons' Tavern in Covent Garden and the Football Association was born, with Morley appointed as the Association's first secretary. Morley drafted the first commonly accepted 'Laws of the Game', which became known as the 'London Rules', and on 19 December 1863 he also played in the first match to be organised under the authority of the FA, a goalless draw between Barnes and Richmond. In 1867 Morley was made President of the FA.

There were some football clubs who effectively opted out of playing by the new Association rules and many of these teams went on to form the Rugby Football Union in 1871. The only club of the original eleven who signed up for the Association in 1863 which still exists today is 'Civil Service FC', who currently play in the Southern Amateur League.

In April 2013 the FA launched a campaign to celebrate its 150th anniversary by appealing to the British public for any information about Morley and his associates, of whom little is known, and to find living descendants to represent their forebears at a ceremony of celebration at Wembley Stadium.

CURSE OF THE CRYPT

HOWARD CARTER (d 1939)

Howard Carter is possibly the world's most famous Egyptologist but will be forever outshone by his greatest discovery, the tomb of the 18th dynasty Egyptian Pharaoh Tutankhamun in the Valley of the Kings, or, as it is known more prosaically, KV62.

Carter had lived and worked in Egypt for more than three decades before making his famous discovery. Starting out at just 17 years of age copying inscriptions, he served a lengthy apprenticeship to become Inspector-General of Monuments in Upper Egypt. But it was under the employ of the 5th Earl of Carnarvon that he was to make his great find.

The prolific Egyptologist Theodore M Davis had excavated more than thirty tombs in the Valley of the Kings and had come across artifacts bearing the name of Tutankhamen. Assuming he had found the tomb of the boy king he considered the valley to be exhausted of archaeology. Carter disagreed and felt that the tomb of Tutankhamun remained undiscovered. He was systematic in his search and thorough with his excavation, but after five years in the Valley of the Kings he had failed to provide his sponsor with the results they had hoped for.

Carnarvon was ready to pull the plug on their endeavours, but Carter convinced him to agree to one last season. After only four days into the final season they had uncovered twelve steps cut into the bedrock leading down to a sealed doorway. The discovery could have been any number of things but Carter dared to believe that this was what he had spent so many years in search of. The entrance was placed under guard whilst Carter made arrangements and summoned Carnarvon from England.

It was on 26 November 1922, and with great anticipation, that they began to open the tomb. In his diary Carter wrote 'With trembling hands I made a tiny breach … I inserted the candle and peered in; as my eyes grew accustomed to the light, details of the room within emerged, strange animals, statues, and gold – everywhere the glint of gold. I was struck dumb with amazement.' When anxiously asked by Lord Carnarvon if he could see anything, Carter could only respond, "Yes, wonderful things." The antechamber of the King's tomb was piled high with treasures, the scale of which had never been seen before. Further rooms led to further treasures and the burial chamber revealed the King's sarcophagus, his solid gold coffin and the now iconic golden funerary mask that has come to symbolise the boy King and the tomb's discovery.

In the aftermath of the First World War, Carter's discovery was pounced upon by a voracious public sorely in need of a good news story. King Tut became a sensation and the world's press reported every last detail. The legend of Tutankhamun even extended its influence to art, fashion and architecture, heavily inspiring the Art Deco movement of the Twenties.

Four months later Lord Carnarvon died suddenly in Cairo, after accidentally shaving an infected mosquito bite, leading many to report that there was an ancient 'Mummy's Curse' being played out against those who had desecrated the royal tomb. Any mysterious happenings or vaguely related deaths were then attributed to the curse. Most of these stories were fabrication and only served to exaggerate the myth and mystery of King Tut.

The man who made the discovery and spent the next ten years working at the tomb, cataloguing and clearing every last find, appeared to have escaped the clutches of the curse, however, having lived for another sixteen years and into retirement. On 2 March 1939, Howard Carter passed away at his home in Kensington and was buried at Putney Vale Cemetery; his epitaph reads, 'May your spirit live, may you spend millions of years, you who love Thebes, sitting with your face to the north wind, your eyes beholding happiness.'

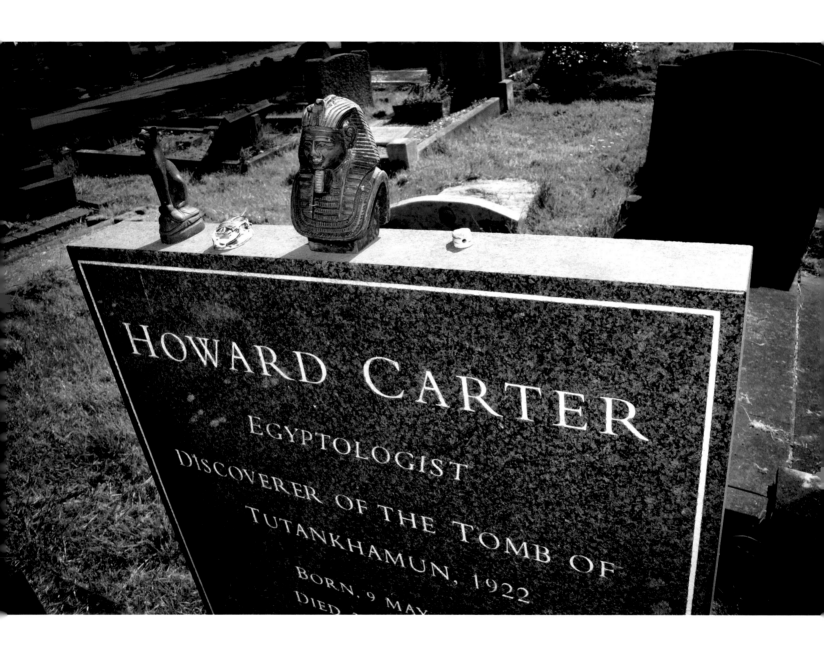

HOWARD CARTER
EGYPTOLOGIST
DISCOVERER OF THE TOMB OF
TUTANKHAMUN, 1922
BORN, 9 MAY
DIED

Brompton Cemetery

WEST
————
LONDON

THE MODERN MORALIST

WILLIAM HOGARTH (d 1764)

Few artists have so vividly captured the essence of contemporary London life, or defined the city's spirit, quite like the celebrated 18th century printmaker William Hogarth. He apprenticed as an engraver and made his name producing satirical studies of the big issues of the day, such as crime and political corruption. Hogarth wasn't afraid to explore the depth of London's humanity and he showed great concern for the improvement of society. These socio-political commentaries proved to be challenging at the time and today they remain as accurate, if amusing, historical records of life in Georgian times.

This was most effectively illustrated by Hogarth's famous engravings of 'Gin Lane' and 'Beer Street' which he made at the time the 'Gin Act' was being administered to curb the illicit sale of spirits. Prints were issued at the affordable price of one shilling each to 'reform some reigning Vices peculiar to the lower Class of People, in hopes to render them of more extensive use'. The melodramatic study compares Gin, the dreaded foreign scourge which had laid waste to the poor of London, with good, hearty English Beer. He set Gin Lane in the parish of St Giles, close to where Tottenham Court Road station stands today, and its alcoholic residents are seen fighting, drunk and dying in the streets as the city crumbles around them. Hogarth pulls no punches and shows the full horror and depravity of the scene, whilst the happy and healthy inhabitants of Beer Street 'quaff thy balmy juice with glee'.

Hogarth became best known for his serialised modern morality tales; these were produced first as paintings, and then sold on subscription as engraved prints. The first of these, 'A Harlot's Progress', tells the sorry tale of a young country girl who seeks employment in London, but is coerced into life as a common prostitute. Similarly 'A Rake's Progress' tells of a young man who squanders his inheritance living the London high life, leaving him a debtor and a madman. Hogarth's prints were a great success and his business flourished, but as a result his work was widely copied. This led Hogarth to lobby parliament for greater legal control over his work and in 1735 he succeeded in bringing about the first copyright legislation to protect artists.

When Thomas Coram opened his Foundling Hospital for the 'maintenance and education of exposed and deserted young children', Hogarth became a founding governor. He and his wife were childless, but during his long association with the charity they fostered many children themselves. Hogarth used his influence to attract the benevolence of fellow artists such as Thomas Gainsborough and Sir Joshua Reynolds, who would donate their work. The hospital accrued such an enviable collection of work that they set up a permanent art exhibition which became London's first public art gallery, and ultimately led to the formation of the Royal Academy of Arts four years after Hogarth's death.

Hogarth's country retreat became a museum in 1904, and much of the surrounding area now appears to have been renamed in honour of Chiswick's favourite son. If you walk from Hogarth's House, down Hogarth Lane, past The Hogarth Business Estate and under the Hogarth roundabout you will find yourself transported from the thunderous traffic of the A4 to the genteel surroundings of the riverside church of St Nicholas. Pride of place there is the tomb of the man himself. Hogarth's epitaph, dedicated by his close friend the actor David Garrick, reads, 'If Genius fire thee, Reader, stay. If Nature touch thee, drop a Tear. If neither move thee, turn away, For Hogarth's honour'd dust lies here.'

THE SAVIOUR OF SOHO

JOHN SNOW (d 1858)

Since the start of the 19th century there have been seven major cholera pandemics which have caused the deaths of millions around the world. It was during the second of these pandemics, which swept across Asia and into Europe, that the disease first reached Britain, in 1831. The first major outbreak in London claimed 6,500 lives and between 1848 and 1854 cholera accounted for a further 25,000 deaths in the capital alone.

It was commonly believed that the disease was airborne and transmitted by smell, which became known as 'miasma' from the Greek for 'pollution'. Leading public health figures such as Florence Nightingale supported this belief and she worked to rid her hospitals of foul odours. There were some who thought that infectious diseases were spread by living bacteria, known as 'germs', but this was not a popular theory. The pioneering physician John Snow was one of the few who supported germ theory and he had the opportunity to put it to the test in 1854.

Another outbreak of cholera had taken hold in the overcrowded and insanitary district of Soho. Snow made local inquiries into the habits of the deceased and produced maps to illustrate the concentrations of the disease. He was able to propose the theory that cholera was spread by contaminated water and he even identified the source of the outbreak as the public water pump on Broad Street (now Broadwick Street). It wasn't just the Soho locals who fell foul of the polluted water, public houses, dining rooms and coffee shops were found to be serving their customers with water from the pump. There was even a case of a woman from Hampstead who had water fetched from this particular pump as she preferred its taste. Snow also found that a brewery of 70 staff, just yards from the pump itself, had recorded no cholera related deaths; none of the men had drunk any infected water as the brewery had its own water supply.

Snow effectively ended the outbreak by having the handle removed from the pump, but 600 lives had already been lost. It was later discovered that the well had been dug dangerously close to an old cesspit and deadly bacteria from human waste had leaked into the water supply. A replica of the pump stands in the same place today, over the road from a pub named in Snow's honour. Snow's discovery was a significant breakthrough in helping to understand the nature of disease, but his theories weren't accepted by Government officials at the time. It was only when better sanitation and Bazalgette's sewerage system were put in place that cholera was eradicated from these shores. Snow did not live to see this happen however; he died at the age of 45 from a stroke during the 'Great Stink' of 1858 and was buried at Brompton Cemetery. His grave, originally erected with his wrong birthdate (1818 instead of 1813), had been restored twice, in 1895 and 1938, before being destroyed in an enemy air raid in April 1941. The replica monument we see today was erected in 1951.

Cholera may have been wiped out in the UK but the disease still persists as a major cause of illness and death in the developing world, affecting millions and killing up to 150,000 people every year.

INDUSTRIAL REVOLUTIONARY
ISAMBARD KINGDOM BRUNEL (d 1859)

The revered engineer Isambard Kingdom Brunel is probably the most famous name in Kensal Green Cemetery, he was one of the greatest industrialists of his age whose work brought Britain to the forefront of global manufacturing and trade, but compared to the high Victorian splendour of many neighbouring mausoleums, the Brunel family tomb is surprisingly modest.

Brunel worked as an apprentice to his father, the French engineer Marc Isambard Brunel, on the world's first underwater tunnel beneath the Thames, but the younger Brunel was caught in a flooding accident and nearly drowned. Whilst recuperating he learned of a competition to design a bridge across the Avon gorge in Bristol. Brunel won second place, but he managed to convince the judges that his bridge should be built and he was awarded the prize. Work began on the Clifton Suspension bridge in 1831 when Brunel was just 25 years old, but due to protracted financial difficulties the bridge was not completed until five years after his death.

Brunel developed strong professional ties with many Bristol businessmen and in 1833 he was appointed chief engineer of the proposed Great Western Railway. It would be Brunel's single greatest accomplishment and become a marvel of the modern age. By today's standards Brunel would be considered a workaholic, he was a perfectionist who displayed an astonishing attention to detail and he also became known for refusing to delegate, preferring instead to get his hands dirty with the rest of his workers.

He was faced with a series of major obstacles in tracing a railway line from London to Bristol and to overcome these Brunel built impressive bridges, viaducts, cuttings and tunnels. The most significant of these engineering achievements were the bridge at Maidenhead, which remains the largest span brick arch bridge to have been built, and the Box Tunnel, which was the longest of its kind, at nearly two miles, and which also claimed the lives of 100 navvies during its construction. The directors of The Great Western Railway made the inaugural journey from Paddington Station to Temple Meads on 30 June 1841 in just four hours.

It was a dream of Brunel's to have passengers travel from London to New York on a single ticket; having completed the first stage between London and Bristol, he began work on the Atlantic crossing with the construction of the steamships *SS Great Western* (1838) and *SS Great Britain* (1843). Brunel's ships successfully proved the viability of a commercial transatlantic service and ushered in a new era of ocean travel.

Brunel's success led to his most ambitious construction project, by far the largest ship to have been built, the *SS Great Eastern*, also known as the 'Leviathan', a magnificent transoceanic steamship that he proposed would journey to Australia and back on a single reserve of coal. The *Great Eastern* was designed to carry 4000 passengers in unparalleled luxury, but from the start the project was beset with problems: financial scandals, a massive fire at the shipyard and several failed launches led many to think the ship was jinxed and contributed to Brunel's untimely death. During its maiden voyage, in September 1859, and just days after Brunel had suffered a stroke, a huge steam explosion in the English Channel blew off one of the funnels, killing five stokers from scalding. Brunel never recovered and died at the age of 53.

Brunel's legacy is vast; he combined ingenuity, passion, theatricality, determination and a genius for engineering that propelled Britain into the industrial age. In a televised BBC poll to find the '100 Greatest Britons', voted for by the British public, Brunel ranked higher than Darwin and Shakespeare, coming second only to Winston Churchill.

COMPUTER GENIUS
CHARLES BABBAGE (d 1871)

It is impossible to imagine a world without the computers on which we rely so heavily today. And it is also difficult to imagine how the idea for such a technology came to fruition in the first place. What mind could conceive of such a thing?

Originally, computers were people, a person who computed calculations. One such computer was the great mathematician and scientist Charles Babbage. Here was a man who studied logarithm tables and dreamed of applying a machine to the task of calculation that would eliminate human error. Babbage could not abide disorder and devoted his life to achieving precision.

In 1822 Babbage presented a paper outlining his 'Difference Engine' to the Royal Astronomical Society. He had conceived a means to calculate algebraic equations known as polynomials. His idea was approved and received significant government funding. It would consist of more than 25,000 parts and weigh 15 tonnes, but in 1834 the work ground to a halt and the machine was never completed. The best mechanical engineering of the day was not sufficient to the task of producing the intricate parts necessary.

Babbage modified his designs and drew up the plans for an altogether more ambitious project. His 'Analytical Engine' could be programmed to specify any calculation required, not just polynomials. The engine would have a 'store', which would act as a memory and a 'mill' that would process the calculation. With this design he created the fundamental features that we see in every computer today. But after failing to deliver his first engine he failed to secure funding on his second and the work also ended before completion.

Further designs were made towards a second difference engine, but he didn't attempt construction. It was these schematics that were discovered in the Science Museum archives and in 1991 the first full size model was completed. It stands at 11ft tall and weighs over two tonnes.

Babbage was a prolific inventor and is credited with an array of wide ranging achievements. He invented the ophthalmoscope; the cowcatcher, for clearing railway tracks; the black box recorder, to be used on trains initially; he advocated decimal currency and was a renowned cryptographer, working with the British military on cracking supposedly indecipherable codes. Babbage also loathed street music and he considered himself persecuted by organ grinders; he estimated that a quarter of his working power had gone to waste with such disturbances. He suffered torment and pushed for legal intervention, eventually succeeding in the introduction of what became known as the 'Babbage Act' by which musicians could be quelled.

Babbage was buried in a modest plot, amidst the high Victorian extravagance of his neighbours at Kensal Green Cemetery, beneath a plain monument of grey Aberdeen granite. He was considered to have one of the greatest minds of his age, but as a consequence of this his brain was removed and preserved for further study; the Victorian's hoped to reveal the secrets of intelligence through dissection. Therefore Babbage went to his grave incomplete. He now occupies three resting places across London, forming what psychogeographers like to call the 'Babbage triangle'. The two hemispheres of his brain remain on permanent display, one half at the Science Museum and the other at the Hunterian Museum a few miles away.

No one at the time could have imagined how Babbage's inventions have helped shape the future of mankind, but with hindsight in a modern computer age we can see just how pioneering he was and truly call him 'the grandfather of computing'.

THE OTHER LADY OF THE LAMP

MARY SEACOLE (d 1881)

Mary Seacole was an unconventional woman, born of Jamaican and Scottish parentage and very proud of her mixed race heritage, she broke racial boundaries and challenged prejudice in Victorian society. Seacole was well educated and travelled extensively; in Panama she established a tumble down two room hotel to accommodate travellers brought by the Gold Rush of 1849, where she also practised nursing in the midst of a cholera epidemic.

At the outset of the Crimean war Seacole travelled to England and applied to join Florence Nightingale's band of military nurses, but was rejected. Undaunted she applied to the War Office to offer her services where she also met with refusal. Undeterred she organised supplies and resolved to open up a 'British hotel' as close to the action as she could get, setting off in January 1855. She built her ramshackle establishment from whatever material was close at hand, such as packing cases and driftwood, and set up close to Sevastopol, near the headquarters of the British army.

Seacole was not a nurse in the traditional sense; she employed Caribbean herbal remedies in her medicine and referred to herself as a 'doctress'. She acted as 'mother' to injured and convalescing British troops who lovingly referred to her as the 'black Nightingale', and she became well known for her excellent cooking and compassionate nursing as well as showing great bravery and courage on the front line. Although she was highly regarded and respected at the time, her 'unofficial' contribution has certainly been overshadowed by that of Nightingale.

When she returned to Britain Seacole was financially ruined, but a fund was set up by her admirers in the military and a few high profile benefits were organised to help aid her plight, which even received the backing of Queen Victoria. In 1857 she published a vivid account of her experiences in the book *Wonderful Adventures of Mrs Seacole in Many Lands*.

Seacole died in obscurity and was buried in an unmarked grave at St Marys Catholic Cemetery in Kensal Green, forgotten for nearly a century. Until, in 1973, her grave was rediscovered and restored, by the British Commonwealth Nurses War Memorial Fund and Lignum Vitae Club, with the addition of a beautifully carved white marble headstone featuring a palm tree of her native Jamaica and a scene from the Crimea.

Following her resurgence as a historical figure a painting, by a little known artist dated 1869, was found in an Oxfordshire car boot sale in 2003 and identified as Seacole by a Crimea historian. In what is thought to be the only known painting of Seacole, she is seen wearing three service medals, the British Crimea, the Turkish Medjidie and the French Legion d'honneur. The painting was bought for £130,000 in 2008 and is now on public display at the National Portrait Gallery.

In response to the BBC's 'Great Britons' survey, Seacole was voted top in a poll to find the 100 most important British black figures. However, her rise to prominence has been criticised by some as an exercise in promoting multiculturalism for the sake of it and that she is in danger of replacing Nightingale in the hearts of the public as the true heroine of the Crimea. In 2012 it was announced that the Conservative Government intended to drop the teaching of Seacole's life and achievements from the national curriculum in favour of more traditional and less ethnically diverse figures such as Oliver Cromwell. But the proposal was met with outrage and the Education Secretary was forced to reconsider when presented with a petition of 36,000 signatures.

HERE LIES
MARY
SEACOLE
1805 ~ 1881

OF KINGSTON, JAMAICA
A NOTABLE NURSE WHO CARED
FOR THE SICK AND WOUNDED IN
THE WEST INDIES, PANAMA
AND ON THE BATTLEFIELDS
OF THE CRIMEA
1854 ~ 1856

THIS GRAVE
A JAMA
ITISH   STORED BY T
RGANISATION I
WAR M   CLUB
                    ND THE
                FIND

SIR . HENRY . COLE . K.C.B

SEASONS GREETINGS

SIR HENRY COLE (d 1882)

The state of this sadly neglected grave does not do its occupant justice for all his achievements. Henry Cole was a lifelong civil servant, but it is not just for his success in promoting the arts and sciences that he is best known, he is also fondly remembered as the man who first introduced Christmas cards to the world.

Cole was an enthusiastic member of the Royal Society of Arts and lobbied to improve standards in design. He secured the support of Prince Albert for a Royal charter and organised an exhibition to showcase the best of British art and manufacturing in 1847.

This was such a great success that it led to a Royal Commission from Queen Victoria and, under the presidency of Prince Albert, Cole organised the first World's Fair in 1851, known as the Great Exhibition. Housed within the magnificent purpose-built Crystal Palace in Hyde Park, it displayed 13,000 exhibits and was attended by six million people.

The enormous profits from the exhibition went into the building of a national museum of arts in South Kensington, which became the Victoria and Albert Museum. Further projects included the building of the Natural History Museum and the Science Museum nearby. Cole was appointed the first director of the V&A when it opened in 1852. He was so influential in transforming the area of South Kensington into a national centre for the arts and sciences he became known as 'Old King Cole'.

Earlier in his career Cole served on a committee with Sir Rowland Hill to reform the postal service. They introduced the penny post in 1840 and the first adhesive postage stamp the Penny Black.

Cole took advantage of this new development and in 1843 he created the first mass-produced Christmas card or, as he advertised his card for sale, 'A picture of Old English Festivity to Perpetuate kind recollections between Dear Friends.' Cole commissioned a thousand lithographed cards which were then hand coloured. The design featured a triptych depicting a family party scene flanked by two acts of charity and the greeting 'A Merry Christmas and a Happy New Year to You'. Only a dozen of these cards are thought to survive. One, sent by Cole himself, was sold at auction in 2001 for a record £22,500.

In an increasingly digital age it is reassuring that the tradition of sending personal handwritten greetings at Christmas is not lost, and it is estimated that over one billion Christmas cards are sent every year in the UK alone.

150 NOT OUT

JOHN WISDEN (d 1884)

His name is synonymous with the game of cricket, not only as one of the great bowlers of the Victorian age but as the founder of the famous reference book *Wisden Cricketers' Almanack*, the oldest continuously published book in the world.

John Wisden played his debut first class match for Sussex in 1845 at the age of 18. He was hardly an imposing figure, as he weighed just 7 stone and stood at 5ft 6in tall, but he proved to be an exceptional fast bowler and earned the nickname 'Little Wonder'. At the height of his career with Sussex in the 1850s it is claimed that Wisden was averaging more than 200 wickets per season, although there are no firm records in place as there was no statistical record book at the time to keep track. The highlight of his career came in 1850 when he bowled all ten wickets of an innings at Lord's.

In 1859 Wisden organised the first ever overseas cricket tour, a pioneering two-month trip of North America that took in eight matches, from Philadelphia and Hoboken to Montreal and Ontario. Cricket in the United States was growing in popularity and if it wasn't for the intervention of the American Civil War less than two years later, it may have become a national sport, but instead it was baseball that proved more popular among the troops on both sides.

Wisden was forced to retire from cricket in 1863 due to rheumatism and the following year he compiled the first edition of his Almanack. His contemporary Fred Lillywhite had for some years published a cricketing guide of sorts,

but Wisden published an authoritative journal of 112 pages, priced at one shilling. Wisden's pages were filled with names and numbers, statistics and lists, not only were there scorecards to act as a permanent record of past matches, but he also included the MCC's revised laws of cricket as well as a variety of unrelated and obscure miscellany, such as notable historic dates, winners of the Epsom Oaks, Cambridge University term times, the relative lengths of British canals and of course the Queen's birthday.

The book has been published every year since, although it came close to missing an edition during World War II when a German bomb hit the Wisden offices. In 1870 Wisden's name was added to the title and in 1938 the book acquired its distinctive yellow cover. The books have also become hugely popular collector's items, with highly-prized original copies of the first edition valued in the region of £25,000.

In April 2013 Wisden published its 150th edition, boasting 1584 pages with comprehensive coverage of every first class match played in every cricketing nation. The book is a must-have accessory for cricket obsessives and still sells around 40,000 copies each year.

Wisden latterly opened a 'cricket and cigar shop' near Leicester Square. He was buried at the fashionable Brompton Cemetery, but his grave was quickly forgotten and remained unmarked for the next hundred years until a granite headstone was erected to mark the centenary of his death in 1984.

RETURN OF THE WILD WEST
CHIEF LONG WOLF (d 1892)

In a quiet corner of a west London cemetery a Native American Sioux warrior lay neglected for more than 100 years until an unlikely discovery led to his celebrated repatriation.

Chief Long Wolf, an Oglala Lakota Indian who fought against General Custer's 7th Cavalry at the Battle of the Little Bighorn in 1876, came to Britain as a performer with the great showman 'Buffalo Bill' Cody. His travelling 'Wild West Show' was a vast production and boasted a troupe of more than 200 performers that included the famous sharpshooter Annie Oakley and, for a brief while, the legendary Chief Sitting Bull. Stagecoach robberies and battles, such as 'Custer's Last Stand', were re-enacted twice daily for an insatiable paying public, with Buffalo Bill playing the part of Custer himself.

During their season at Earl's Court in 1892 Long Wolf, who was the oldest of the performers, died of pneumonia at the age of 59. An autopsy revealed that his body was covered in old battle scars from bullet wounds and sabre cuts.

Long Wolf had expressed a wish to be buried in his native land, but his wife demurred when she realised there was a good chance he would be buried at sea during the long voyage back. Instead, Buffalo Bill gave him a prestigious burial within Brompton Cemetery's grand circle colonnade, his headstone emblazoned with a wolf. The plot cost the equivalent of half the average annual wage at the time.

It was the determination of Elizabeth Knight, a Midlands housewife, who had read about the life and death of Long Wolf a century later, which brought about the final chapter in his story. The fact that he was lost and alone in a strange land struck a chord with her and she set out to find his burial site, scouring graveyards, looking for the wolf carving.

On making her discovery at Brompton she contacted a Dakota newspaper to help trace any surviving relatives and found the Chief's granddaughter Jessie Black Feather. There was no question that Long Wolf should return to his homeland and permission was granted by the Queen for his remains to be exhumed. Also found with Long Wolf were the bones of a small child, thought to be those of Star Ghost Dog; a 17-month-old girl who fell from her mother's arms whilst she performed on horseback during the Earl's Court show.

In September 1997 Chief Long Wolf began the long journey home; his spirit was finally laid to rest at Wolf Creek Cemetery in the Pine Ridge Reservation of South Dakota.

DEEDS, NOT WORDS

EMMELINE PANKHURST (d 1928)

The right to vote is a concept that we take very much for granted today, but it is only thanks to generations of political activists that we have that right at all. In 19th century England the entire political system underwent a major overhaul, for centuries voting had been the privilege of an elite few, rather than a democratic right for all. The disenfranchised working classes fought for the vote and brought about the Reform Act of 1867, which saw that all householders were given the ability to vote, but the Charter didn't go far enough and excluded the right for women.

The Women's Suffrage movement grew from a network of campaign groups across the country. In Manchester the suffragist Emmeline Pankhurst and her husband Richard founded one such group, the 'Women's Franchise League', in 1889. Pankhurst had the ability to express her ideas in words that all classes could understand and this gave her great power to influence others. For many years they held meetings, published pamphlets, gathered petitions and lobbied Parliament, but the restrained approach yielded little in the way of progress. Richard was a prominent campaigner, and he even authored the first women's suffrage bill that went before Parliament, but he died from a gastric ulcer in 1898.

Pankhurst moved to London to intensify her campaign and with the support of her daughters, Christabel, Sylvia and Adela, she went on to form the 'Women's Social and Political Union' in 1903, a suffrage group that advocated direct action. The group gained notoriety for a succession of minor offences and some activists were sent to prison whilst campaigning for Women's votes; members were arrested for civil disobedience, smashing windows and assaults. Pankhurst herself was first arrested, for obstruction, while attempting to deliver a petition to the Prime Minister at the Houses of Parliament, and was sentenced to six weeks in prison.

The cause earned itself a good deal of publicity and they became known in the Press as 'Suffragettes', the term was most likely intended as disparaging but the Suffragists seized on it and turned it to their advantage. Pankhurst's Suffragettes redoubled their efforts knowing that the nuisance of their imprisonment brought with it valuable column inches and they went out seeking deliberate arrest, but Pankhurst always maintained that they were forced to become 'law-breakers' as a means to becoming 'law-makers'.

Their heightened militancy culminated in two high profile events that were to change the face of the Suffragette movement. Firstly, in June 1913 the activist Emily Davison was killed after she stepped in front of King George V's horse as it raced in the Epsom Derby. The second act of protest, came in March 1914 at the National Gallery when Mary Richardson attacked a priceless painting, the 'Rokeby Venus', with a meat cleaver.

The Suffragettes came up against widespread ridicule and fierce opposition but they also won some prominent political support, most notably from the founder of the Labour party Keir Hardie. At the start of the First World War Pankhurst suspended all suffrage activism and called for her supporters to redirect their efforts against the Germans.

Following the War an act of Parliament in 1918 granted women over the age of 30 the ability to vote and in 1928 the 'Equal Franchise Act' finally granted women the same voting rights as men. Pankhurst knew she had finally achieved her goal, and just two weeks before the act was made law, she died at the age of 69. She was buried beside the Central Avenue of Brompton Cemetery beneath a Red sandstone Celtic cross.

LOONY TUNES

SCREAMING LORD SUTCH (d 1999)

Screaming Lord Sutch became one of the most familiar faces of British politics and is fondly remembered for having subverted election nights for almost four decades. He is recognised by the *Guinness Book of Records* for having contested and lost more British elections than anyone else, but he is also acknowledged as the longest-serving political leader in the UK.

Inspired by 'Screaming' Jay Hawkins, David Sutch changed his name to 'Screaming Lord Sutch, 3rd Earl of Harrow' and began his wild public life in the early wave of British Rock and Roll with his band 'The Savages'. The band were well known for their 'Shock and Roll' horror shows and they released a succession of singles throughout the sixties, including 'Jack the Ripper' in 1963, which was banned by the BBC.

Sutch recorded his debut album 'Lord Sutch and Heavy Friends' in 1970 with some high profile contributions from the likes of Jimmy Page and John Bonham of Led Zeppelin, guitarist Jeff Beck and Jimi Hendrix's bass-player Noel Redding. With such a reputable gathering of talent the record promised so much, but in fact it is widely regarded as one of the worst albums ever made and has become something of a cult classic for that reason alone.

Sutch continued to record and perform music throughout his life, but an eccentric political career beckoned. He first ran for election as the 'National Teenage Party' in 1963, with a single-issue campaign to reduce the voting age from 21 to 18, contesting the seat made vacant by John Profumo following his sex scandal. Sutch became a familiar sight on election nights in his trademark top hat and leopard-skin jacket and he made a name for himself running as the 'Sod 'Em All Party' and the 'Go to Blazes Party' before founding the 'Official Monster Raving Loony Party' in 1983 with the slogan 'Vote for Insanity, you know it makes sense'. Sutch contested 39 elections and would throw victory parties the night before polling day knowing he would inevitably lose. The bookmakers William Hill once offered shorter odds on Elvis Presley crashing a UFO into the Loch Ness Monster than Lord Sutch ever becoming Prime Minister.

The Monster Raving Loony Party was an entertaining addition to the political spectrum, and became popular for some of its more ridiculous Manifesto pledges, such as making winter shorter, by abolishing January and February, replacing the national anthem with 'Do the Funky Gibbon' by the Goodies or promising heated toilet seats to pensioners.

He was a constant thorn in the side of mainstream politics and made a repeated mockery of the democratic process. Sutch ran against Margaret Thatcher for her Finchley seat during the 1983 General Election and even joined the Conservative Party at one stage with the intention of challenging the Prime Minster for her leadership, but his greatest triumph came in 1990 at the Bootle by-election when he beat Lord Owen's Social Democratic Party, contributing to the party's demise just a few days later.

Throughout his career Sutch had fought a long battle with manic depression and this worsened considerably following the death of his mother in 1997. Just two years after her death and under threat of impending bankruptcy Sutch took his own life at his home in Harrow. He was buried with his mother in Pinner New Cemetery and his epitaph reads 'A Lord without peer, Sutch is the way it was with him, and Sutch is why he'll always be with us'.

St Patrick's Roman Catholic Cemetery, Leytonstone

EAST&CITY
LONDON

✠ hic iacet Raherus Primus Canonicus et Primus Prior hujus Ecclesiæ

MEDIAEVAL HEALTH SERVICE

RAHERE (d 1144)

Occupying a peaceful corner behind the market of Smithfield is the 12th century church of Saint Bartholomew the Great, considerably dwarfed by its neighbouring establishment, St Bartholomew's hospital. Within the chapel there survives the wonderful mediaeval tomb of their founder, Rahere.

Legend has it that Rahere popularly entertained the court of King Henry I as a jester, gaining himself a position of influence and respect. A poem by Rudyard Kipling suggests that he was 'feared by all the Norman Lords, for his eye that pierced their bosoms, for his tongue that shamed their swords.' Disaster plunged the royal household into deep mourning in 1120 when the King lost his son and heir in the sinking of the *White Ship*, off the coast of Normandy. It is said that, such was his grief, he never smiled again.

Rahere found himself without a role to play amidst such misery and undertook a pilgrimage to Rome. It was during his travels, whilst suffering from malaria, that St Bartholomew appeared to Rahere in a fevered vision. Rahere prayed for his recovery and vowed that if he regained his health he would build a church and hospital on his return.

King Henry granted him a Royal charter in 1123 and work began at Smoothfield, beyond the city wall. The priory hospital had not been completed by the time of Rahere's death in 1144 and his tomb was built into an arch in the presbytery. The original 12th century recumbent likeness of Rahere is attended by two kneeling canons reading verse from *Isiah*, at his feet an angel bears the coat-of-arms granted to him by the King.

A section of the tomb was opened during restoration in 1866 and the sandaled feet of Rahere were exposed; the custom being for Augustinian monks to be buried in their sandals. In 1890 it was discovered that the sandals had been stolen and were presumed lost. But the relics were eventually found, hidden in the north transept, yards from the tomb itself.

As Britain's oldest hospital, St Bartholomew, or Barts, as it became known, has been at the forefront of pioneering modern medicine for over 400 years. A considerable pedigree, which includes William Harvey, who discovered the circulation of blood, James Parkinson, researcher of the shaking palsy, Elizabeth Blackwell, the country's first female doctor and John Down, the man who described Down's Syndrome.

These days the hospital's services care for more than 750,000 patients a year. In the hospital's cancer treatment and research centre there is a ward dedicated to the revered and benevolent Rahere.

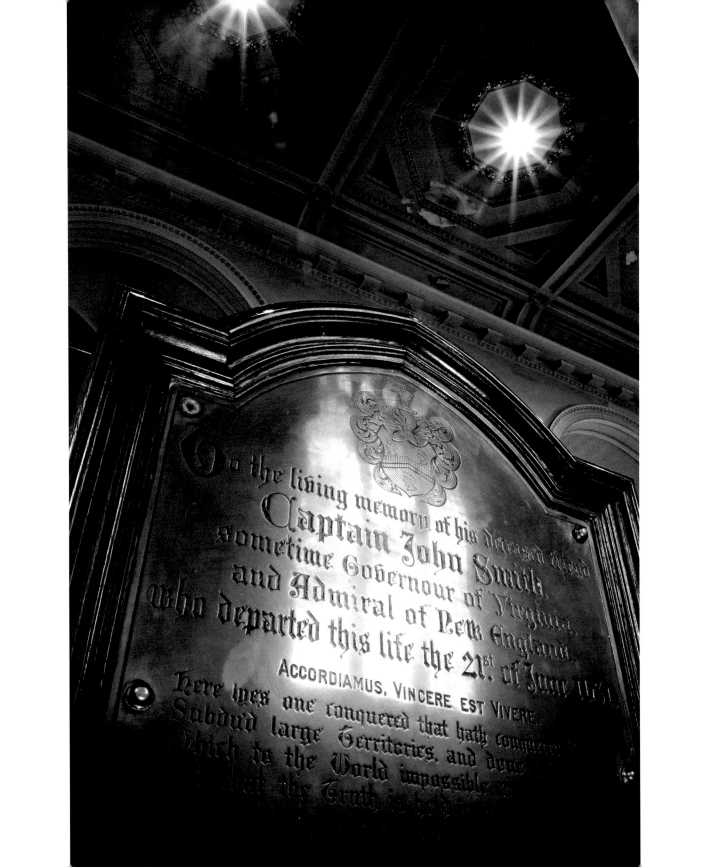

OLDEN VIRGINIA

JOHN SMITH (d 1631)

For centuries European explorers sailed across the Atlantic Ocean seeking to establish trade routes and colonies. Norse adventurers preceded these forays by a good 500 years but failed to make permanent settlements. The first to claim the 'New World' was Christopher Columbus, in 1492. He landed in Central America and there initiated the process of Spanish colonisation. John Cabot, an Italian explorer under English patronage, sailed the latitude from Bristol becoming the first European to discover North America, landing in Newfoundland in 1497.

It took more than 100 years for the English to establish a colony in North America, founding Jamestown, Virginia, in 1606. A Royal charter was granted by King James I establishing the 'Virginia Company of London' which was responsible for funding and supporting the development of the English settlers.

Among those aboard the first three ships was Captain John Smith, a colourful character, valiant soldier and seasoned seaman. Before sailing for the Americas he had been variously employed as a mercenary in war, fighting for the French, Dutch and Austrians, as well as being sold into slavery by Ottoman Turks.

The Jamestown colonists faced harsh conditions and as they gradually encroached on Native American lands they suffered attacks from the surrounding Algonquian tribes. Powhatan, a tribal chief and confederacy leader, captured Captain Smith in 1607. He condemned Smith to be ritually executed but the Chief's young daughter Pocahontas dashed forward pleading for clemency, saving him from certain death. 'At the minute of my execution' he wrote, in a letter to Queen Anne, 'she hazarded the beating out of her own brains to save mine.'

A period of co-operation followed during which Pocahontas acted as an intermediary between her father's tribe and Smith's settlers. Smith, elected as the Governor of Jamestown, showed great leadership and made an effort to learn some of the native language, using diplomacy and trade to advance his community. He organised the colony with discipline warning that "He who does not work will not eat". The Natives soon began to feel threatened by the expansion of Jamestown. Fearing for their land, hostilities commenced once more. Captain Smith was severely injured by a gunpowder explosion during an incursion and was forced to return to England for medical attention. He never returned to Virginia.

Smith encouraged many of his countrymen to become pioneers themselves by joining the colonies in America. 'Here every man may be master and owner of his owne labour and land.' He offered freedom, liberty and wealth to the industrious. Some years later he gave the name New England to the lands north of Virginia, earning him the title 'Admiral of New England'.

Spending the remainder of his life writing books back in England, Smith spun subjective, swashbuckling yarns of his adventures, leading many critics to disbelieve his heroic embellishments. Whether or not Pocahontas actually saved his life, is still a matter for debate. The 1995 animated Disney re-telling, *Pocahontas* propagates the tale, whilst erroneously casting Mel Gibson as Captain Smith in a romantic love affair with the teenage Princess.

Smith died in 1631 and was buried in the south aisle of St Sepulchre's Church at the junction with Newgate prison, now the Old Bailey. His epitaph begins, 'Here lies one conquer'd that hath conquer'd Kings, Subdu'd large Territories, and done things Which to the World impossible would seeme.' A grand stained glass window erected in the 1960s commemorates the achievements of the great Captain.

PILGRIM'S CHOICE

JOHN BUNYAN (d 1688)

A charming oasis set amongst the towers of concrete and glass of London's square mile is the historic cemetery of Bunhill Fields. Dating back to Saxon times, Bunhill (the name is thought to be a derivation of 'Bone Hill') has now found itself enveloped by London's crowded financial district.

The ground at Bunhill had never been consecrated for religious burials and so appealed to those with independent religious beliefs. It was so highly regarded as a Nonconformist site that it induced both John Wesley to found his original Methodist chapel and George Fox to establish a Quaker burial site on either side of the cemetery.

After squeezing in excess of 123,000 burials into such a small site, the last interment at Bunhill took place in 1854 and the area was landscaped into a public space. Pride of place at the centre of Bunhill today is situated a grand monument that marks the burial site of one of the 17th century's most celebrated writers, John Bunyan.

Bunyan was born to an illiterate, Bedfordshire tinker and received little in the way of education. At the age of 16 he joined the Parliamentary army and fought with Oliver Cromwell's 'Roundheads' (a derisory term to describe the cropped bowl shaped hairstyle of 'Puritan' men) against the Royalist Cavaliers in the first English Civil War. In the army Bunyan was exposed to uncensored Puritan propaganda and he learnt much about new religious ideas and the divisions in the Anglican Church.

After leaving the army he too became a tinker, but as he travelled from village to village, repairing pots and pans, he began to give talks about the bible and share his religious beliefs. He joined a Bedford Baptist church in 1653 and began lay preaching some time later. Following the restoration of Charles II's monarchy the law forbade unlicensed preaching - fearful that it may stir up rebellion again. Bunyan was arrested and imprisoned in November 1660. His freedom was offered to him on the condition that he stopped preaching illegally, but the strength of his convictions caused him to be incarcerated for 12 years. He wrote many theological books while in prison, even an autobiography, but it was in 1676, during a further six-month period of confinement for the same violation, that he began to write his most famous work.

The Pilgrim's Progress From This World, To That Which Is To Come to give it the full title, is a religious Christian allegory that symbolises the passage from a world of sin to a heavenly afterlife. By using simplistic prose that was easily understood and accessible to all, Bunyan explained the morality and ideology of the Bible in its most basic terms.

The story follows its hero Christian as he leaves The City Of Destruction to undertake a pilgrimage to the Promised Land of his deliverance, the Celestial City. The journey of life takes him through the Valley of Humiliation and into the Slough of Despond, and confronts him with the temptation of Vanity Fair. But he eventually succeeds in his noble quest, if only with the cooperation and encouragement of his friends, Evangelist and Good Will.

The clarity of its message was the key to the book's everlasting success; *The Pilgrim's Progress* was one of the first books to be produced for a mass audience and is now considered one of the most important works of English literature. In over 300 years it has never been out of print and has been translated into more than a hundred languages.

It is said that many of the early pilgrims who settled in the United States took only two books for comfort, the Bible and *The Pilgrim's Progress*.

SAMVEL PEPYS
born Feb\[!] 23,1632.
died May 26,1703.

ERECTED 1883 BY PVBLIC SVBSCRIPTION MAINLY OWING
TO THE EFFORTS OF HENRY BENJAMIN WHEATLEY 1838-1917
D C L F S A EDITOR OF THE COMPLETE EDITION
OF THE DIARY

NOTES ON A SCOUNDREL

SAMUEL PEPYS (d 1703)

Of all the great figures in history, be they royalty, celebrity or statesman, it is curious to imagine that the one person we probably know the most about is a 17th century civil servant by the name of Pepys.

Between the years 1660-1669 Samuel Pepys kept a personal diary, which was never meant for public consumption, just one man alone with his thoughts and observations laying bare his soul with brutal honesty. Written in a form of shorthand, the bound volumes were discovered, deciphered and first published in 1825.

It was Pepys' personal accounts of historical events, at such a turbulent time in British history, that have cemented the diaries in the consciousness of the public. He witnessed the massive upheaval of Civil War leading to the Restoration of the Monarchy and he also wrote vivid, first-hand accounts of the Plague of 1665 followed by the Great Fire of London the year after.

Pepys had a curious mind and took the greatest pleasure in the minutiae of his own existence, fascinated by himself and the world around him. In its very mundanity the diary reveals so much more than was ever intended. We are granted intimate familiarity with Pepys' friendships, personal finances and insecurities, his New Year resolutions 'abstaining from plays and wine', even his bowel movements.

His exuberant libido, extra-marital affairs and petty jealousies led to a fractious relationship with his wife Elizabeth. On being discovered red-handed in the throws of an indiscretion with the young maid, Deb Willet, he described Elizabeth as 'struck mute' with anger.

At the age of 15 Pepys took time off from school to attend the execution of Charles I in 1649 and in April 1661 he witnessed the coronation of Charles II. That evening, with the yeoman of the King's wine cellar, Pepys 'drank the King's health till one of the gentlemen fell down stark drunk'.

At the outset of the plague in April 1665 Pepys wrote, 'Great fears of the Sickenesse here in the City. God preserve us all'. He moved Elizabeth out of the city to Woolwich where he spent much of his time avoiding the pestilence and recording its onslaught.

In the early hours of 2 September 1666 Pepys was woken by his maid with news of a great fire. He reasoned that the fire was far enough away and of little threat so he returned to his slumber. As he went about his business later that morning the full magnitude became apparent, 'a most horrid malicious bloody flame, churches, houses, all on fire and flaming at once.' So great was his fear that Pepys busied himself with removing everything of value; his money and gold secured, he then set about burying his wine and a Parmesan cheese in the garden.

As well as serving as an MP and President of the Royal Society, Pepys is also known for the major reforms he introduced as a Naval Administrator, bringing about the provision for sailor's pensions and payments for widows. By standardising ship types and food rationing at sea, he turned an inefficient navy into a professional force, earning him the epithet 'father of the modern Royal Navy'.

Pepys held a close connection with St Olaves Church in Seething Lane, referring to it as 'our own church'. He regularly attended sermons in the Navy Office gallery, which he'd had constructed. When Elizabeth died, in 1669, Pepys commissioned a monument to her, which was placed high on the North wall opposite her husband's pew. Upon his death Pepys instructed that he was to be buried beside his wife in the chancel vault. The existing Victorian monument to Pepys in the south aisle marks the doorway through which Pepys accessed his pew.

METHOD MAN

JOHN WESLEY (d 1791)

The Methodist movement, often referred to as the Wesleyan revival, began with the evangelising brothers John and Charles Wesley. Born to a Lincolnshire clergyman they were faithful with their bible study and true to its teachings. The use of the term 'Methodist' came about in 1732 as a disparaging word to describe the brothers and their bible reading friends while studying at Oxford. Fellow students made fun of their 'Holy Club' and the methodical way they regularly observed fasting and prayer. Their Methodism became a symbolic reaction to the increasing apathy of the Church of England and its exclusion of the poor.

After completing his degree in Classics John Wesley took Holy Orders and was made a deacon of Christ Church Cathedral. He conducted sermons and held tutorials at the college, but the more he examined the ideology of his own faith the more evangelical his teachings became and the more he was criticised for it; parents feared their children might become indoctrinated by his ardent preaching.

In 1735 Wesley started to travel, spreading word of his Methodist beliefs; he began as an American missionary, in the Colony of Georgia. During his voyage a great storm broke the ship's mast and, as most of the passengers flew into a panic, Wesley noticed that a band of devout Moravian settlers calmly prayed for deliverance. He believed that their faith was greater than his own and the experience became an important influence on his Methodist theology.

He achieved little success in the Americas and returned to England to begin an intense campaign of evangelism, preaching mainly to the poor and forgotten in many industrialised areas where the Church of England feared to tread. Wesley once said, "I look upon all the world as my parish", and he travelled anywhere he would have an audience. Wesley was an influential speaker and he delivered his teachings with passion and eloquence, challenging people's view of Christianity; he performed thousands of sermons in the open air and set up hundreds of chapels, building up a huge following.

Wesley was concerned about social justice and urged his followers to work to improve the lives of others, encouraging them to "Make all you can, save all you can, give all you can." He campaigned for prison reform and earned a reputation as a pioneer of universal education.

The Methodist Church established hospitals, soup kitchens, orphanages and schools as well as undergoing extensive missionary work, bringing Wesley's influence to every corner of the globe.

Wesley's famous chapel opened on City Road in 1778 and it still serves as the focal point for world Methodism today. The grade I listed chapel maintains a thriving congregation and is a place of pilgrimage for many millions of modern Methodists.

Wesley continued to give sermons until right up until his death at the age of 88. He died in the house he built beside the chapel and was buried in the chapel garden which, sadly, is now overlooked by a rather incongruous modern office block. He was a poor man when he died, having lived a humble life, and it is said that when he passed away all he left behind were a library of books, a well-worn gown and the Methodist Church.

ENGLAND EXPECTS ...

HORATIO NELSON (d 1805)

Directly beneath the massive dome of St Pauls Cathedral, in the crypt, there lie the remains of Britain's greatest naval leader, Vice-Admiral Horatio Nelson, 1st Viscount Nelson, the hero of Trafalgar.

By the time of Nelson's great victory at Trafalgar in 1805 he'd already earned quite a reputation as a naval commander and strategist and was riding high on the back of a string of famous victories. He had been badly wounded in the Battle of Santa Cruz de Tenerife against the Spanish in 1797, and had lost his right arm. But undaunted, he spent much of the intervening years pursuing Napoleon's fleet, winning a decisive victory over the French in 1798 at the Battle of the Nile, and the Danish at the Battle of Copenhagen in 1801, but it was at Trafalgar that he was to lose his life and achieve immortality.

Napoleon had combined his French and Spanish fleets at Cadiz in south-west Spain and numbered 33 ships to Nelson's 27, and as they departed for the Mediterranean Nelson's fleet was waiting, near the Cape of Trafalgar. During the battle Nelson was shot by a sniper and mortally wounded, but he survived for long enough to learn that the battle had been won. His body was transported back to London, preserved in a cask of brandy.

The funeral on 9 January 1806 was to be a huge public event, grandstands were erected along the procession route and preparations were made for a full state funeral, a rare and prestigious accolade.

Following an earlier victorious campaign, Nelson had been presented with a section from the mast of a French ship and he had commissioned an undertaker to make the timber into a coffin, which awaited him in London. The fatal bullet was removed by a doctor and Nelson was prepared for his final voyage. After lying in state for three days the coffin was carried on a funeral barge up the Thames from Greenwich to Whitehall, and then he was taken through the streets on the back of a horse-drawn funeral cart which had been specially designed to look like his ship, the *Victory*. Tens of thousands of mourners gathered for a glimpse of the endless procession that was led by the Duke of York as it made its way to St Pauls Cathedral for the funeral service.

It had been decided that to carry Nelson's coffin down the stairs to the crypt for interment would not be appropriate for the occasion so a hole was made in the floor and the coffin was lowered into his tomb. The granite base to the tomb is actually where Nelson's coffin lies, not as is generally thought, in the black sarcophagus which was added some years later.

The marble casket was originally commissioned by Cardinal Wolsey nearly 300 years earlier, but by the time of Wolsey's death he had fallen out of favour with his King, Henry VIII, and he never received the grand burial he had hoped for. It was eventually re-appropriated for Nelson's tomb and topped with a marble cushion on which now sits Nelson's viscount's coronet. The finishing touch to the tomb was the elaborate mosaic floor which is rich in detail and contains numerous naval motifs, with the addition of Nelson's famous rallying cry prior to the victory at Trafalgar, 'England expects every man to do his duty'.

In 1838 a committee of MPs was formed with the intention of erecting a monument to Nelson. The site, a former Royal stableyard, was chosen and a public square was laid out in front of the new National Gallery building, which had just been completed. Nelson's 170ft column and 18ft sandstone statue were raised in 1843, and Trafalgar square was opened to the public the following year.

POETIC VISIONARY

WILLIAM BLAKE (d 1827)

The 1960s were not kind to the memory of one of London's most famous sons. In the same decade the birthplace of William Blake in Soho was demolished to make way for a residential tower block and his gravesite was lost when his stone at Bunhill Fields was moved to make way for a lawn.

Blake was, in the truest sense, a real Londoner; he spent almost his entire life in the capital working as an artist, poet and printmaker with such an idiosyncratic and prodigious talent that, although he achieved little success during his lifetime, he is he now thought of as one of the most visionary and influential figures in both art and literature.

The young Blake had early ambitions as an artist and served as an apprentice to an engraver, eventually setting himself up in business as an illustrator and printmaker with his wife Catherine. Blake invented a method of printing, known as 'relief etching', which enabled him to combine words and images on the same page and create the beautifully self-illustrated 'illuminated poetry' that he is famous for.

Blake claimed to have seen visions since he was a boy and these fed his imagination for religious imagery; his work was deeply spiritual and often mystical, but also extremely radical for the time. In 1789 and 1794, he published the illustrated volumes *Songs of Innocence* and *Songs of Experience* the two 'Contrary States of the Human Soul'. The poems were simple in style, almost childlike, but displayed a profound depth and complexity and dealt with some of the most topical issues of the day such as child labour, poverty and social justice, leading many to believe in retrospect that he was one of the most original thinkers of his time.

Blake is perhaps best known today as the author of the short poem 'And did those feet in ancient time', which was set to music by the composer Sir Hubert Parry in 1916, to 'brace the spirit of the nation' during World War I, and it became the anthemic hymn 'Jerusalem'. The poem originally served as a simple preface to Blake's epic poem 'Milton' but has since become one of the best loved British hymns. It was chosen to be sung during the wedding of the Duke and Duchess of Cambridge and, such is its patriotic appeal, has become a permanent fixture during the 'Last Night of the Proms' alongside 'Land of Hope and Glory' and 'Rule, Britannia!'

Blake died in poverty in 1827 whilst carrying out a commission to illustrate Dante's *Divine Comedy*, it is said that he spent his last shilling on a pencil so that he could carry on working. Catherine was so committed to her husband's work that, even after his death, she continued to produce his works and was believed to 'consult' with him on matters of business.

The plain memorial stone we see today at Bunhill was erected at his original grave in 1927 by the Blake Society on the 100th anniversary of his death, but after the cemetery suffered bomb damage in World War II the stone was moved roughly 20 metres away to sit beside the monument of Daniel Defoe. The 'Friends of William Blake' group was formed in 2005 to petition for an appropriate monument to mark the exact location of Blake's grave.

THE ANGEL OF THE PRISONS

ELIZABETH FRY (d 1845)

Elizabeth Fry was born into two of the great early Quaker banking dynasties; her father John Gurney had founded Gurney's of Norwich, and her mother was part of the Barclay banking family. She met fellow Quaker, Joseph Fry, a member of the Fry's confectionary family, and the two married in 1800, setting up home in Plashet, East London.

Fry was true to her Quaker beliefs and placed great value in modesty and virtue. Although she and Joseph had 11 children, she would devote much of her spare time to helping local people in need. She organised collections for the poor, paid visits to the sick and taught local children to read. But it was after being asked by a Quaker missionary to witness the conditions at Newgate Prison that she decided to devote her life to prison reform.

She was horrified by what she saw. Fry found that female prisoners were forced to sleep on stone floors without nightclothes or bedding, hundreds of women had to cook, wash and sleep in the same cells, in cramped and insanitary conditions. Although some women had been found guilty, often for the slightest of crimes, many others were still waiting to be tried and others still were joined by their children who had nowhere else to go. The prison system appeared to deal in harsh revenge rather than offer redemption, punishing inmates by stripping them of their humanity.

Fry began to pay regular visits to the women of Newgate Prison. She supplied them with clothes and bedding and established a school in the prison. She spent many nights there and even invited members of the nobility to do the same so they could see conditions for themselves. In 1821 she enlisted the help of friends and founded the 'British Ladies' Society for Promoting the Reformation of Female Prisoners', which is thought to be the earliest known national women's organisation. The society lobbied parliament for improvements and she became the first woman to speak before the House of Commons when she presented evidence on the appalling conditions of the country's prisons. She became something of a celebrity and was greatly admired by Queen Victoria, who would often donate to Fry's causes.

It wasn't enough that she should reform the prison system but Fry also established night shelters for the homeless, worked for the abolition of slavery and opened a training school for nurses. Fry's nursing programme went on to inspire Florence Nightingale and her work in the Crimean War.

On her death Fry was buried at the Friends' burial ground in Barking. However, her gravestone no longer marks her resting place. The burial ground was bought by Barking Council and turned into a public garden, whilst Fry's headstone was relocated to a Quaker Cemetery in Wantage.

In 2002 Fry was immortalised on the reverse of the new edition £5 note, she is pictured reading to inmates at Newgate Prison, set against a design of prison keys. Since Florence Nightingale, who featured on the £10 note up to 1994, no other woman besides the Queen had featured on an English banknote. To restore balance the Bank of England drew up a shortlist of notable women, which included the National Trust founder Octavia Hill, author Jane Austen and poet Elizabeth Barrett Browning. Fry was perhaps a surprising and obscure choice, certainly when compared to such noteworthy luminaries as Darwin, Dickens and the Duke of Wellington. There are in the region of one billion £5 notes in circulation, yet Elizabeth Fry remains a strangely unfamiliar face to the majority of us. She is due to be replaced in 2016 by Sir Winston Churchill.

THE RIPPER'S LAST STRIKE

MARY KELLY (d 1888)

The story of the Whitechapel Murderer, more popularly known as Jack the Ripper, is one of the most famous ever told, but at its heart there remain the forgotten victims of a brutal and murderous campaign of terror. The romantic notion of a cloaked and shadowy figure stalking the dark and misty streets of Victorian London has spawned a multitude of dramatic retellings, propagating the legend and distorting the facts.

If it wasn't for the deadly intervention of the Ripper Marie Jeanette Kelly would have lived out her life in obscurity, rather than being the victim of one of the most famous and blood thirsty murders in history.

By the time of Kelly's murder, the east end of London was reeling from the shock of four brutal murders in two months. The murders of Mary Ann Nichols, Annie Chapman, Elizabeth Stride and Catherine Eddowes followed the same pattern; the victim was a working as a prostitute, her throat had been cut and she had been mutilated, leading many to believe that the serial killer was a surgeon or butcher, possibly well-educated or even aristocratic. Suspicion was rife, locals lived in fear, speculation as to the killer's identity was out of control and the police were widely criticised for failing to catch the culprit.

On 9 November 1888 Kelly's savagely mutilated body was discovered in her quiet backstreet room in Spitalfields, off the notorious Dorset Street, and it seems the Ripper had spent much of the night at his work, judging by the extent of the injuries she sustained.

She was unrecognisable; her throat had been slashed so deeply her head had almost been severed; her internal organs had been removed and distributed about the bed, and her heart was missing. Her landlord John McCarthy described the horrific scene as "more like the work of a devil than the work of a man."

Kelly was to be the last of the Ripper's victims; why he ceased his campaign of terror at this point will never be known, but it's the greater mystery of the killer's identity which has baffled historians and sleuths for more than a century. It's the ultimate whodunit, but without a definitive culprit, although there have been hundreds of theories and potential suspects.

Kelly was interred in a public grave in St Patrick's Cemetery in Leytonstone; no member of her family could be traced to attend her funeral. The stone that marks her grave is modern and bears the touching inscription from a poem by Goethe, 'None but the lonely hearts can know my sadness.'

In modern day London the streets around Whitechapel and Shoreditch have changed beyond compare in the intervening years but the Ten Bells pub on Commercial Street which is central to the Ripper story, and was regularly frequented by Mary Kelly, has little changed and continues to attract hordes of tourists and Ripper walking tours.

THE ART OF REBELLION

SIR JOHN EVERETT MILLAIS (d 1896)

In 1848 three idealistic young Royal Academy students, John Everett Millais, William Holman Hunt, and Dante Gabriel Rossetti founded The Pre-Raphaelite Brotherhood (PRB), the first British 'modern art' movement. The Pre-Raphaelites fundamentally believed that the overriding influence of Italian artist Raphael had had a detrimental effect on academic tradition, and that the 19th century art establishment had become formulaic and staid as a result. They agreed to rebel against conventional art theory and looked instead to the early Renaissance masters, before Raphael, for inspiration.

They were very much the 'enfants terribles' of their day, similar in some respects to the likes of Tracey Emin or Damien Hirst, and their early works received a largely hostile reception. In particular, Millais' controversial painting 'Christ in the House of His Parents' was widely criticised as blasphemous when it was first exhibited in 1850. The press was scathing in its reviews but this only served to give the Pre-Raphaelites fame and notoriety. They found an unlikely ally however when the famous art critic John Ruskin leapt to their defence praising their unconventional approach and 'truth to nature'. Gradually Ruskin's support led to their acceptance and, inevitably, the Pre-Raphaelites became part of the establishment themselves.

One of the best loved and well known Pre-Raphaelite works of art is Millais' 'Ophelia', painted in 1852. Taken from Shakespeare's *Hamlet*, the painting depicts the tragic heroine Ophelia singing as she drowns in a stream. Millais spent five months braving the elements on a riverbank painting the richly detailed and heavily symbolic natural elements and then caused his model, the Pre-Raphaelite muse Elizabeth Siddal, to catch pneumonia as she posed in a bathtub for days on end. Sir Henry Tate bought the painting in 1892 and it was included in his 'gift to the nation' when he opened the Tate Britain in 1897, where the piece remains.

Millais developed a close friendship with his supporter and patron John Ruskin and his wife Effie modelled for Millais during his painting of 'The Order of Release'. Effie's marriage to Ruskin was unhappy and unconsummated and as they spent their sessions together she and Millais gradually fell in love. Effie had her marriage annulled and went on to marry Millais causing a huge public scandal. They had eight children together, but the demands of family life caused Millais to drift away from the Brotherhood with which he made his name, and he began to paint more commercial work. Subsequently Rossetti took the Pre-Raphaelites in a more aesthetic and romantic direction, influencing the likes of Edward Burne-Jones, William Morris and the Arts and Crafts Movement.

Millais was often criticised for his own change in direction and was accused of 'selling out' when his painting 'A Child's World', of his young grandson blowing bubbles from a bowl of soap suds, was bought by the Pear's Soap company and used in a famous advertising campaign. The young grandson, William Milbourne James, went on to become an Admiral in the Royal Navy, but he would never shake off the nickname 'Bubbles'.

Shortly before his death Millais was made president of the Royal Academy, finally becoming head of the establishment he had started out with as a precocious and prodigious young talent. He is buried in 'Artists Corner' in the crypt of St Paul's Cathedral surrounded by many of his contemporaries. Beside him lies one of the nation's favourite landscape artists JMW Turner and close by are his friend and fellow Pre-Raphaelite Holman Hunt and the famous Royal Academy presidents Sir Joshua Reynolds and Sir Edwin Landseer Lutyens.

THE GREAT DEFENDER

BOBBY MOORE (d 1993)

One of the most iconic images in British football is that of the great Bobby Moore holding aloft the Jules Rimet trophy, as he is carried on the shoulders of his jubilant team mates after leading his team to victory in the 1966 World Cup final. The England captain is widely regarded as one of the most legendary players the game has seen, but to be hailed by Pele as the best defender he ever played against is possibly the greatest accolade.

Moore was born in Barking and began his career at West Ham United, playing his first match in September 1958. He made his England debut in May 1962 and the national manager Walter Winterbottom was so impressed by the rookie defender that he played him for the duration of that year's World Cup tournament in Chile, where they lost in the quarter finals to the eventual winners Brazil. Just a year later he was made England captain at the age of 22 and remains to this day the youngest man to have held that position. In 1964 the indomitable Moore was treated for testicular cancer just weeks after winning the FA cup with West Ham.

When accepting the job of England manager in 1963 Alf Ramsey boldly declared that England would win the World Cup in 1966, a prediction that most people thought highly unlikely considering Brazil's dominance of the game at that time. But the majestic England team breezed through the group stage and reached the final without conceding a single goal, such was Moore's leadership and dominance in defence. The historic 4-2 win over West Germany remains one of the country's greatest sporting triumphs.

Moore again captained England as they defended their title in the 1970 World Cup in Mexico, but they lost out to West Germany who sought revenge in the quarter finals. He eventually retired in 1973 with 108 caps, a record only beaten by Peter Shilton and David Beckham.

After a few years of illness Moore succumbed to bowel cancer at the age of 51. His funeral was held at Putney Vale Crematorium followed by an interment at the garden of remembrance in the City of London Cemetery just over a mile from Upton Park, the home of West Ham where he played for 16 years. A memorial service held at Westminster Abbey was attended by all of his World Cup winning teammates. Moore's widow Stephanie founded the Bobby Moore Fund shortly after his death to raise public awareness of bowel cancer and money for research into new surgical techniques and treatments; the fund has so far raised over £18million for Cancer Research UK.

In 2007 a twice life size bronze sculpture of Bobby Moore by Philip Jackson was unveiled outside the newly rebuilt Wembley Stadium in a commanding position looking along Wembley Way with an inscription that reads, 'Immaculate footballer, Imperial defender, Immortal hero of 1966, National Treasure, Lord of the game, Captain extraordinary, Gentleman of all time.'

BROTHERS IN ARMS

RONALD & REGINALD KRAY (d 1995 & 2000)

The Kray twins were the most notorious gangsters of their day and came to symbolise the seedy underworld of London's East End during the swinging sixties. They led the lives of celebrities, but with their gang 'The Firm' they also bred a reputation for violence.

Reggie, the older brother by ten minutes, and Ronnie spent their formative years as promising young boxers; they were inseparable, tough and ambitious. Prior to becoming career criminals, the twins often had brushes with the law. In 1952 they were amongst the last people to be imprisoned in the Tower of London when they were caught avoiding National Service. The twin's route into organised crime was through extortion and protection rackets. They ran a snooker club on the Mile End Road, recruited a crop of local hard men and began to expand their criminal empire.

They opened their own nightclub, the 'Double R', in Bow Road in 1957, but the Krays enjoyed their heyday whilst running a Knightsbridge gaming club called 'Esmeralda's Barn', where they lived the glamourous playboy lifestyle and mixed with a class of people they had never come across before, brushing shoulders with stars such as Judy Garland and Frank Sinatra. The pair seemed untouchable.

Reggie married Frances Shea in 1965 but, unable to stand the pressure of the gangster life, she left him after eight weeks and committed suicide. Reggie was so distraught at Frances' death that he went on a spree of violence which culminated in the murder of Jack 'The Hat' McVitie, an odd job man for The Firm. His body was never found. Ronnie was even more unpredictable than his brother; he was mentally unstable and his legacy of violence led him to murder another local gangster, George Cornell, an associate of the Krays' rival gang

the Richardsons. In March 1966 Ronnie walked calmly into Whitechapel's Blind Beggar pub and, as the jukebox played the Walker Brothers' 'The Sun Ain't Gonna Shine Anymore', he shot Cornell through the forehead in front of a room full of eyewitnesses, apparently upset at being called a 'fat poof'.

The Krays activities had long been under police scrutiny, but it took a dedicated Scotland Yard investigation led by Inspector Leonard 'Nipper' Read to bring the twins to justice. Eventually Read built up enough evidence to charge the twins and on 8 May 1968 he conducted a coordinated raid with more than 100 policemen, arresting the Krays as well as a further 15 members of The Firm. Their trial at the Old Bailey was the longest of its kind in British criminal history and the sentences handed down were the longest ever given for murder; the Kray twins were sentenced to life imprisonment, with a minimum term of 30 years.

The twins were allowed out of prison in 1982 to attend the funeral of their mother Violet; they arrived for the service handcuffed to prison guards and were not permitted to attend the interment at the family plot in Chingford Mount Cemetery. Ronnie died from a heart attack at Broadmoor Hospital in 1995 and Reggie was released from prison in 2000 to receive treatment for bladder cancer; he died three months later. They were buried together beside their mother.

It was the end of an era for the East End; Reggie's funeral brought Bethnal Green to a standstill, with more than 100,000 mourners lining the streets to see the funeral procession of 16 black limousines pass by. The Sinatra song 'My Way' was played during his service at St Matthew's Church and his horse-drawn hearse, pulled by six black plumed stallions, was decorated with flowers that spelled the words 'Free At Last'.

Poets Corner, Westminster Abbey

CENTRAL
LONDON

THE OLD BARD OF WESTMINSTER

GEOFFREY CHAUCER (d 1400)

Geoffrey Chaucer is considered one of the most important writers of the English language. He was the finest poet of his day and has been described as the man who first 'found' the English language.

Chaucer moved in the highest social circles; he worked in the service of Lionel of Antwerp and later John of Gaunt, both sons of King Edward III, and his wife Philippa was lady-in-waiting to the Queen, Philippa of Hainault. It is thought Chaucer's first major poem *The Book of the Duchess* was written to commemorate John of Gaunt's wife Blanche when she died in 1368. He was highly regarded by the court of King Edward III and Chaucer served his sovereign well, notably as Clerk of the King's Works, Comptroller of Customs in London and as a Member of Parliament. On St George's Day in 1374 the King granted Chaucer a gallon of wine a day for the rest of his life, believed to be one of the first Royal endorsements of the arts and a precursor to the position of Poet Laureate.

In 14th century England the main written languages were Latin and French, but Chaucer chose to write in the language he spoke and in doing so he popularised the use of written vernacular English. The phrase 'through thick and thin', for example, was first written by Chaucer as 'thurgh thikke and thurgh thenne'. Thousands of the words he used, although popular in contemporary spoken English, were written for the first time by Chaucer and are still in everyday use today; such as 'accident', 'funeral', 'galaxy', 'horizon', 'outrageous', 'scissors' and 'vacation'.

His best known work is undoubtedly *The Canterbury Tales*. The story follows a group of pilgrims as they journey together from the 'Tabard Inn' on Borough High Street in Southwark, to the shrine of the 12th century martyr St Thomas Becket at Canterbury Cathedral. The collected tales are written in the form of a story-telling contest, each member of the group competing to win a free meal on their return to the Tabard. Chaucer wrote each tale from the point of view of the storyteller, and in doing so he paints a vivid picture of mediaeval society, encompassing all walks of life and class divisions, from the gallantry of the Knight and the romance of the Squire to the low morals and debauchery of the Cook and Miller.

Copies of *The Canterbury Tales* were reproduced by hand copyists and these manuscripts were circulated among Chaucer's friends and distributed to members of the Royal court. The wider population did not get to enjoy Chaucer's masterpiece until long after his death. It wasn't until 1476 when William Caxton set up his printing press in Westminster that he published the first edition of *The Canterbury Tales*, the first book in English to be printed in England. A rare copy of this first edition was sold at auction by Christie's in 1998 for $7.5 million.

Chaucer had long held close associations with Westminster, he worked as Clerk of Works to the palace of Westminster and shortly before his death he is believed to have been living as a tenant of the Abbey. When he died in 1400 he was buried in the south transept with a simple lead plate for a memorial. The marble tomb we see today was installed more than 150 years later by an admirer. Although Chaucer was the first poet to be buried in Poet's Corner, the tradition of writers, poets, playwrights and actors choosing to be buried or memorialised here only took off two centuries later, after the Elizabethan poet Edmund Spenser was buried close to Chaucer's tomb.

TUDOR TRAILBLAZER

SIR WALTER RALEIGH (d 1618)

Walter Raleigh was an aristocrat and explorer and one of the most prominent and fashionable men of his day. He is famously remembered as the chivalrous gentleman who laid his velvet cloak over a muddy puddle to save Queen Elizabeth I from dirtying her feet, but regardless of whether there is any truth in the tale, or if it's just a popular myth, Raleigh was indeed a favourite of the Queen and one of her most popular courtiers.

It was Elizabeth's father Henry VIII who had broken from the Roman Catholic Church, and Raleigh, a prominent protestant who had played a part in the suppression of an Irish rebellion, gained favour with the Queen for his anti-Catholic views and was handsomely rewarded with vast estates in the Province of Munster.

Raleigh used his influence and wealth to sponsor the establishment of a colony in America. The expedition landed in 1584 and Raleigh named Virginia for his 'Virgin Queen', but the early settlement at Roanoke Island was abandoned just a few years after being founded. The colonists did not return from Virginia empty handed though; they brought with them the crops that would make Raleigh famous for introducing to Britain, tobacco, potatoes and maize. In fact Raleigh became such an avid smoker of tobacco himself that he is considered chiefly responsible for popularising the pastime amongst the fashionable elite of Elizabethan society. It is said that a servant once doused Raleigh in water while he smoked, thinking that his master was on fire.

Raleigh was knighted by the Queen in 1585, but his popularity wasn't to last. He fell in love with one of the Queen's ladies-in-waiting, Bess Throckmorton, and in 1591 they were married in secret without having asked the Queen's permission. Bess soon fell pregnant and the jealous Queen was so enraged she incarcerated the couple in the Tower of London.

In 1603 Raleigh was implicated in a plot to oust the Queen's successor, King James I. Based on flimsy evidence he was found guilty and sentenced to a gruesome death, but with the King's intervention this was instead reduced to life imprisonment and he was again sent to the Tower. Raleigh was eventually released in 1617 to undertake a voyage to Guyana in a quest to find the fabled 'City of Gold', El Dorado, but only on the condition that he and his men avoid any conflict with the Spanish. Raleigh was an old man at this stage and he waited at base camp in Trinidad whilst his son Watt travelled up the Orinoco River in search of untold riches. However, the expedition attacked a Spanish outpost and Watt was killed in battle. King James received a bitter complaint from the Spanish ambassador and, when he returned to England in 1618, Raleigh was subsequently beheaded for disobeying orders.

Public support was greatly in favour of the heroic Raleigh and his execution was carried out quickly at Old Palace Yard. His headless body was hurriedly buried at the nearest church, within the chancel of St Margaret's beside Westminster Abbey, rather than at his wife's Surrey estate in Beddington as she had requested. Raleigh's severed head was embalmed and given to Bess as a grisly keepsake. Legend has it that she kept it by her side in a leather bag for nearly thirty years until her death, whereby their son, Carew, took possession, and it was only following his death that the famous head is thought to have been returned to its rightful resting place at St Margaret's.

IN HER OWN WRITE

APHRA BEHN (d 1689)

Little is really known about the details of Aphra Behn's life and she remains something of a mysterious figure, but her achievements and literary legacy are enormous. She was by no means the first female English writer but she was the first woman to earn her livelihood from writing.

Behn was born Aphra Johnson and took the name of her Dutch husband, who after a brief marriage left her widowed at the tender age of 25. Mrs Behn was held in high regard by the court of King Charles II for her wit, judgment and strength of character and she was employed as a spy in Antwerp during the Anglo-Dutch War, on reconnaissance under the codenames 'Agent 160' and 'Astrea'. It is thought that Behn communicated specific intelligence of a proposed attack on the Thames estuary, but her information was ignored. The ensuing attack in June 1667 on the Medway docks led to the loss of 13 English ships. Behn became disillusioned with her employers and returned to London, but to make matters worse the King refused to pay her for her labours and she wound up in a debtors' prison.

This event was to signal a turning point in Behn's life. On her release from prison she vowed to become financially independent and pursued a career in writing. Her first play, *The Forc'd Marriage*, performed in 1670, was a success and there followed more plays and volumes of collected poetic work. In 1677 she wrote and staged her best known play *The Rover* for which the famous actress and King's mistress, Nell Gwyn played a starring role.

Behn did not re-marry, preferring instead to enjoy her own sexual freedom, and this was reflected in the liberating nature of her poetry, much of it erotically charged and some in exploration of her bisexuality. In the 17th century any sexual activity between women was unheard of, so it wasn't even thought of as particularly sinful or taboo at the time. She was widely criticised for her explicit writings though, and one male contemporary even dubbed her the 'punk poetesse' (punk in this instance meaning 'whore') for her seemingly immoral and ambiguous verse. Not only was she seen as breaking boundaries in poetry but also in her personal life, leading to public ridicule as well as admiration. She wrote about fairness in love and the liberties that men take, at a time when there was no gender equality.

Perhaps Behn's most significant work was the novel *Oroonoko* published in 1688, which tells of the Ghanaian Prince Oroonoko and his ill-fated love for Imoinda, amidst the backdrop of a slave revolt on a sugarcane plantation in Surinam. Not only was this ground-breaking, in that it portrayed black African slaves sympathetically, but it is also thought to be one of the earliest examples of a novel - prose fiction with a linear plot, written in English.

Behn's writing was largely ignored as indecent by the prudish scholars of the 18th and 19th centuries; her work only became properly appreciated in the more liberated 20th century and she is now hailed as an icon of feminist literature. Virginia Woolf paid tribute by writing, 'All women together ought to let flowers fall upon the tomb of Aphra Behn, for it was she who earned them the right to speak their minds.'

Behn is buried in the east cloister of Westminster Abbey, close to Poet's Corner, beneath a black marble stone. Her epitaph, believed to have been written by her bisexual lover John Hoyle, reads, 'Here lies a proof that Wit can never be Defence enough against Mortality.'

FORCE OF NATURE

SIR ISAAC NEWTON (d 1727)

This magnificent monument to one of the world's greatest scientific minds is set in the ornate choir screen and stands in pride of place in the heart of Westminster Abbey's nave. Isaac Newton was one of the leading figures of the 'Scientific Revolution', an intellectual movement which signalled a move away from the 'Age of Faith' towards a more enlightened and scientific approach to understanding the world.

Newton first came to prominence whilst studying at Cambridge University and in 1667 he was made a fellow of Trinity College. He displayed an early genius for mathematics and developed important theories in algebra and calculus, but his life's studies were far broader and included theology, alchemy, natural philosophy, economics and astronomy. In 1668 he built the first reflecting telescope and researched the properties of light, developing the theory of colour based on the optical spectrum.

It was in his most famous work *The Principia* (Mathematical Principles of Natural Philosophy), published in 1687, that Newton first stated the universal laws of motion which would go on to form the basis of classical mechanics. Newton explained the forces that govern momentum and inertia and he demonstrated the workings of the natural world based on sound mathematical principles, including the movements of the earth, moon, and sun, but most significantly Newton outlined the law of gravity.

There is an element of truth in the well-worn legend that an apple falling from its tree brought about Newton's discovery of gravity. Newton had been struggling to formulate his gravitational theory for many years and it is thought he was inspired by the sight of the apple and wondered why it would always descend towards the ground, not sideways or upwards, but towards the earth as if there was a force that attracted the apple. This event came to illustrate his theory perfectly and he proposed the universal law by which all matter holds this attractive force. The famous apple tree that survives at his former home of Woolsthorpe Manor, in Lincolnshire, is protected by the National Trust and receives many thousands of visitors every year.

In 1699 his patron at the time was the Chancellor of the Exchequer and he employed Newton in an honorary post as Master of the Mint, but Newton was serious about his work and set about reforming the British currency system. He was elected President of the Royal Society in 1703, a position he held until his death, and was knighted by Queen Anne in 1705. When Newton died he was afforded the highest honour and was granted a state funeral.

Newton's actual grave is situated on the floor just in front of his monument. The marble monument, created in 1731, shows the classical figure of Newton reclining on a sarcophagus which depicts cherubic boys diligently employed in a variety of Newton's scientific pursuits. His arm rests upon his life's works and he appears to be gesturing towards a mathematical design held by two more winged cherubs; mounted on a pyramid above him is a celestial globe, detailed with the constellations of the zodiac. The Latin inscription translates, 'Here is buried Isaac Newton, Knight, who by a strength of mind almost divine, and mathematical principles peculiarly his own, explored the course and figures of the planets, the paths of comets, the tides of the sea ... mortals rejoice that there has existed such and so great an ornament of the human race!'

CABINET OF CURIOSITY

JEREMY BENTHAM (d 1832)

In the south cloisters of University College London's Bloomsbury campus can be found one of London's most bizarre and surprising sights, it's not a grave as such, but does serve as the final resting place of the college's spiritual founder, the Utilitarian philosopher Jeremy Bentham.

Bentham was a political theorist and radical thinker who was such a precocious talent as a youngster that he started studying at Oxford University at the age of 12. He was set on a course for a career in law, but instead chose to set about reforming the law. Bentham was years ahead of his time and advocated sexual equality and rights for women; he promoted the idea of representative democracy; called for the abolition of slavery; and was the first to argue for homosexual law reform. In his *Introduction to the Principles of Morals and Legislation* Bentham also introduced the idea of animal rights by stating, 'The question is not, can they reason? nor, can they talk? but, can they suffer?'

Bentham died at the ripe old age of 84. His will stipulated that his body should be dissected; his skeleton stripped of its flesh, then reassembled and dressed in his own clothes. He was padded out with hay and placed on display, positioned in a seated position, as requested, in a wooden cabinet that he called his 'Auto-icon'.

Bentham also proposed that his head be preserved by mummification but unfortunately this didn't go as well as hoped and any semblance of a human expression on his face had been stripped away to such an extent that it horrified onlookers and could no longer be put on show. Eventually it was substituted with a modelled wax head. For some years though, Bentham's real head was kept inside the cabinet, but it became a target for mischievous students; a rival college stole the head in 1975 and demanded a £100 ransom for its return, whilst another story suggests that the head had been used a football.

One of Bentham's more radical philosophies was that the dead should be more useful to the living and he asserted that this method of 'human taxidermy' could become a fashionable substitute for conventional burials and possibly even replace the need for statues, 'so now may every man be his own statue'. Not surprisingly this didn't catch on and Bentham's auto-icon remains the only one of its kind.

In 1976 Bentham was brought out of his cabinet to attend a meeting on the 150th anniversary of the college; the minutes record him as being 'present, but not voting'.

Conservators working on the auto-icon in 2002 found an infestation of carpet beetles, known as 'woolly bears'. His bones were also found to be discoloured and greasy and one of his ankles appeared to have been broken, but after a catalogue of repairs he is now in the best state of preservation he has ever enjoyed and will continue to startle unsuspecting Freshers for years to come.

GRAND DESIGNS

SIR JOHN SOANE (d 1837)

Nestled snugly in the ancient churchyard of St Pancras Old Church, sandwiched between the Eurostar and east coast main lines leaving King's Cross station and St Pancras International and the borders of Camden, lies the mausoleum of the famed architect Sir John Soane. The monument was originally designed and built by Soane to his wife Elizabeth on her death in 1815 and is one of only two grade-1 listed tombs in London; the other belonging to Karl Marx at Highgate.

Soane's name may not be immediately familiar to most, but the fruits of his labours are well known to all. He is best known as the architect of the Bank of England. He was appointed in 1788 and spent the next 45 years rebuilding the Bank, the pride of his life's work. The straight lines of his Neo-Classical style were to become the blueprint for 19th century commercial and industrial architecture. Unfortunately, in the 1920s, in what has been described as 'the greatest architectural crime of the twentieth century', Soane's old bank was demolished to make way for a modern ten-storey office space, seven storeys above ground and three below. Only the fortified curtain wall of Soane's original building remains.

Another of Soane's great achievements was the Dulwich Picture Gallery in South London, the world's first purpose-built public art gallery. The gallery opened its doors in 1817, and Soane's much admired design, incorporating a suite of gallery rooms illuminated from above by skylights, became the model for displaying art collections and has influenced the architecture of many art galleries since.

As Soane's business flourished he began to collect art, antiquities and architectural salvage, gradually filling his home in Lincoln's Inn Fields with items such as the great sarcophagus of Egyptian Pharaoh, Seti I, which he bought in 1824 when the British Museum chose not to buy it, Roman bronze statues and marbles, neo-classical sculptures, Renaissance artefacts, paintings by Canaletto and the eight original paintings that make up William Hogarth's famous morality tale *A Rake's Progress*. In order to house this growing obsession he bought the two neighbouring houses and developed them into what is now considered one of London's best kept secrets, The Soane Museum.

Soane's influence over architecture may have been far reaching but it was the design of his own grave that inadvertently inspired one of Britain's most enduring design icons of the 20th century, the distinctive red telephone box. Giles Gilbert Scott, grandson of the eminent Victorian architect George Gilbert Scott, based the design for his 1924 K2 telephone kiosk on Soane's ornate stone tomb. Scott was a great admirer of Soane's work and borrowed the tomb's idiosyncratic domed canopy as the basis for his kiosk. The immediately recognisable telephone box was once a familiar site across the country and one of the most characteristic symbols of the British Isles.

KING OF COMEDY

JOSEPH GRIMALDI (d 1837)

Beside the bustling Pentonville Road near King's Cross is the churchyard of St James, re-named as 'Joseph Grimaldi Park' by Islington council in honour of its most famous resident, the father of modern clowning.

Born to Italian ballet performers in 1778, Grimaldi made his stage debut aged three at Sadler's Wells theatre and went on to become a national institution. Although modern clowns are now closely associated with circus, Grimaldi performed in pantomime and variety theatre. In his most common guise he sported a white face and rouge cheeks, developing the comedy, physicality and expressionism of the harlequin character, giving rise to the popular term 'Joey'.

Grimaldi was widely regarded as an innovative comic genius and had audiences rolling in the aisles for more than 40 years. Not only was he trained as a singer, dancer, acrobat, juggler and mime artist, but he was also adept at building sets and arranging choreography. His performance range went far beyond comedy though and he was always well received in drama and farce as well as the occasional Shakespearian role. His immense natural acting ability could reduce an audience to tears.

Grimaldi signed a three-year contract with the Covent Garden theatre in 1806, receiving £1 a week, rising to £3 in the third year. The pantomime that made him a household name was the first production of the French fairy tale *Mother Goose* in which he played Harlequin. Grimaldi stole the show and it ran for three months, making it the most successful production of its kind.

Such was Grimaldi's fame that a young Charles Dickens was approached to write his biography. Dickens received the manuscript of memoirs, whilst his early work *Oliver Twist* was still being serialised in *Bentley's Miscellany*, and was paid an advance of £300. The book was originally credited to Dickens' pseudonym, Boz.

Grimaldi made his farewell performance at the Drury Lane theatre in 1828. He fell into ill health and lived a retirement funded by his admirers and contemporaries. Barely able to walk, his body was wrecked by the strain of years of physical performance. His remaining years were spent at the Cornwallis Tavern in Pentonville where each night the landlord would carry him home.

In 2010 artist Henry Krokatsis created an installation that invited the public to dance on Grimaldi's grave. A series of bronze tiles set into the ground played musical notes when stepped on, allowing the dancer to play the tune to Grimaldi's popular song 'Hot Codlins'.

An annual memorial service, at All Saints Church in Hackney, is attended by clowns in full costume from the world over in Grimaldi's honour.

REVOLUTION IN WAX

MARIE TUSSAUD (d 1850)

The ubiquitous queues that form along Marylebone Road in the summer months are a tribute to the continuing popularity of one of London's most visited tourist destinations. The waxwork museum of Madame Tussauds is famous the world over for allowing its guests the opportunity to walk among the stars of stage, screen and sport, and to meet notable figures from history. But how an 18th century French entrepreneur came to create such an unlikely institution, during the most turbulent period in French history, is a macabre tale of remarkable fortune and blind ambition.

Born Anna Maria Grosholtz, the young Marie began to learn the art of wax working from her mother's employer, Dr Phillippe Curtius, a Swiss physician who modelled wax to illustrate anatomy. As Curtius began to display his models audiences flocked to witness such curiosities. Marie began to work for Curtius whilst still a teenager and the first subjects she created in wax were the philosophers Voltaire and Rousseau, major figures of the Enlightenment. It was these famous likenesses that brought her to the attention of the royal court of Louis XVI and she was invited to teach art at the Palace of Versailles. But in 1789 Marie found herself caught in the middle of the French Revolution. As Abolitionists sought to destroy the monarchy her close royal ties landed her in prison, facing execution by guillotine, the fate that met so many thousands during the 'Reign of Terror'. Marie's head was shaved in preparation, but at the last minute one of the Reign's ringleaders, Jean-Marie Collot d'Herbois, who supported the work of her mentor Dr Curtius, saved her from the guillotine and organised for her release.

Following her lucky escape, Marie was unwillingly employed to make wax death masks of recently beheaded victims. Her grisly job was to search through bloody piles of disembodied heads, many of whom had been her friends, to find suitable subjects to cast and model. These included King Louis XVI and his wife Marie Antoinette, who were both charged with treason and executed in 1793. A year later the radical leader of the Revolution, Maximilien Robespierre, fell foul of his own guillotine after his 'National Convention' tried him for tyranny. His death mask remains on display to this day at Tussauds in London.

In 1795 Dr Curtius died, leaving his entire wax collection to his protégé. That same year she married Francois Tussaud, giving the museum its famous name. Marie Tussaud began to tour with her collection and came to London in 1802. As the Napoleonic Wars were being fought throughout Europe she chose to stay in Britain, and for the next 33 years she toured the length and breadth of the country with her travelling museum. Tussaud would never return to France or her husband again, and in a letter to Francois she wrote, 'My enterprise became more important to me than returning to you.'

The lengthy tour finally came to rest in 1835, and she set up a permanent exhibition at premises on Baker Street. Many of her death masks formed what would become her most popular exhibit, the Chamber of Horrors. The last model Tussaud made, in 1842, was a self-portrait, which now greets visitors at the entrance to the museum. At the old age of 88 Madame Tussaud passed away. She is buried in the vault beneath St Mary's Catholic Church in Chelsea.

Madame Tussaud's Waxwork Museum relocated to its current premises in 1884 and now operates globally across nine sites in five countries, from Hollywood to Hong Kong.

O pour charity pray for the repose of the Soul of

Mad.^{me} Marie Tussaud.

who departed this Life April the XV MDC....

Aged XC Years.

Requiescat in Pace

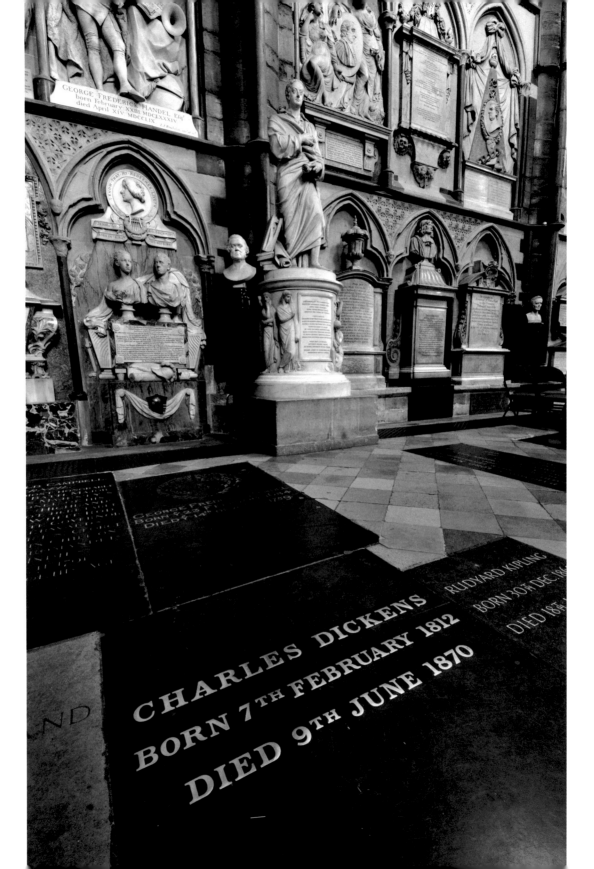

GEORGE FREDERICK HANDEL Esqr.
born February. XXIII MDCLXXXIV.
died April XIV MDCCLIX.

CHARLES DICKENS
BORN 7TH FEBRUARY 1812
DIED 9TH JUNE 1870

RUDYARD KIPLING
BORN 30TH DEC. 186
DIED 18TH

OUR MUTUAL FRIEND

CHARLES DICKENS (d 1870)

Charles John Huffam Dickens led a perfectly normal and happy childhood in rural Kent up to the age of 11, but his father soon found himself in a debtor's prison in Southwark and for a while his family joined him there too. Plunged into poverty, the Dickens family sought accommodation in Camden Town and the 12-year-old Charles was employed at a boot polish factory labelling jars where he would endure long days of rat infested filth and humiliation for only a few shillings per week.

These experiences would go on to become a profound influence on his later writing, but this also led to his tireless campaigning to improve the living conditions of the working classes.

Dickens began writing as a reporter and, although he excelled in journalism under the pen name 'Boz', he was asked to write a series of comedic sketches which would go on to become his first serialised novel *The Pickwick Papers* in 1837. He followed this with his most famous work *Oliver Twist* which he completed at just 26 years old. With just two novels behind him, Dickens' success was assured, but for such an influential figure in English literature it is perhaps surprising that Dickens wrote only 15 books.

Some of the most memorable characters to have graced English literature have been conjured by the imagination of Dickens, from the irrepressible Wilkins Micawber and the unforgettable Ebenezer Scrooge, to the withered Miss Havisham and villainous Uriah Heep; but the most vivid and grotesque character to emerge throughout Dickens' writing was the city of London itself, leading many to describe the Victorian capital as 'Dickensian'.

With the publication of his famous novella *A Christmas Carol* in 1843, we can thank Dickens for transforming the way we celebrate Christmas today. Not only did the book popularise the use of the phrase 'Merry Christmas', but the story proved so popular that Scrooge's redemption effectively redefined the 'spirit' of Christmas and this brought with it a festive revival. Christmas celebrations previously mixed religious tradition with sobriety and reflection, but the Victorian revival, which also saw the first Christmas Trees introduced by Prince Albert and Henry Cole's first Christmas cards, focused on generosity, goodwill and merriment.

Dickens' outstanding popularity took him all over America and Europe for a series of reading tours and it was this exposure that led to him becoming one of the most recognised men of his day and, more than a century before the concept even existed, the first true celebrity.

In 1865 Dickens was returning from Paris when he was involved in a serious rail accident on a viaduct at Staplehurst in Kent. Dickens' carriage was one of the few to stay on the tracks when the train derailed and he leapt to the aid of the wounded. Ten people were killed in the disaster and it seems the traumatic episode affected him very deeply as his writing became less prolific.

Dickens was in the process of writing *The Mystery of Edwin Drood* when he suffered a stroke at his home in Higham; he didn't regain consciousness and died the following morning at the age of 58. By the time of his death half the *Edwin Drood* serialisation had already been published in six instalments, but the mystery was compounded by the fact that the identity of the murderer was never revealed, leading to much speculation since.

It had been requested by Dickens himself that he should receive a simple funeral in Rochester without fuss or monument, but the weight of public grief led him to be buried at Westminster Abbey in Poets Corner. Dickens was buried in secret during a private family ceremony attended by only 12 people, but his grave was left uncovered for a further three days so that mourners, who filed past his grave in their thousands, could pay their respects.

THE EVOLUTION REVOLUTION

CHARLES DARWIN (d 1882)

Charles Darwin was one of the most famous, controversial and influential figures of the 19th century whose earth-shattering scientific discoveries have transformed our understanding of the world.

Fresh from Cambridge University Darwin joined a scientific survey expedition as a self-financing 'gentleman naturalist' aboard *HMS Beagle*. The voyage was scheduled to last for two years but actually took five. After a series of delays the *Beagle* finally set off in 1831 and carried out exhaustive studies of South America before returning to Britain across the Pacific Ocean via Tahiti, New Zealand and Australia. Darwin's interest was primarily geological and he obsessively collected and recorded as many fossils and specimens as he could, but it was at the Galapagos Islands in the Pacific that he made his ground-breaking observations.

Around the archipelago Darwin collected bird specimens and noticed that each island had sustained its own unique variation of Galapagos finch. He recorded twelve different species of finch, each displaying characteristics that appeared to have evolved in isolation, depending on the bird's main food sources.

Darwin had left Britain a 22-year-old college graduate and, having circumnavigated the globe, returned an accomplished naturalist, becoming something of a celebrity in scientific circles. He catalogued his specimens and spent the next 20 years developing the theory of evolution by the process of natural selection, whereby all species, of animal or plant, are descended from common ancestors and those best adapted to their environment are more likely to survive and reproduce. He illustrated this by proposing a branching pattern he called the 'Tree of Life'.

Darwin had nearly completed his research when the naturalist Alfred Russel Wallace also came forward with a similar idea, so the two men jointly announced their discovery in 1858. The following year Darwin published the book that would revolutionise the natural sciences and change the world, *On the Origin of Species by Means of Natural Selection, or the preservation of favoured races in the struggle for life*, to give it the full title.

It is fair to say that before Darwin published *On the Origin of Species* it was commonly believed that the world had been created by God in seven days as described in the Book of Genesis. Darwin's theory of evolution therefore was immensely controversial as it essentially disproved the Bible, provoking a hostile reaction from many leading figures in the Church. There were others who also objected to Darwin's assertion in his book *The Descent of Man* that humans shared a common ancestry with apes. The Prime Minister, Lord Palmerston, proposed that Queen Victoria should bestow a knighthood upon Darwin, but the appointment was blocked by one of Darwin's most vocal opponents, Bishop Samuel Wilberforce.

Since returning from his great voyage Darwin had suffered with poor health and he became reclusive, shying away from publicly debating his theories; choosing to spend his days conducting experiments and writing a variety of detailed analyses on subjects as diverse as orchids, earthworms and barnacles.

Darwin lived and worked at Down House near Biggin Hill, his home for 40 years, and it was understood by his family that when he died he would be buried in the local churchyard. But on hearing the news of his friend's death the president of the Royal Society, William Spottiswoode, wrote to the Dean of Westminster requesting that Darwin be buried at the Abbey. Despite his agnostic views, Darwin was so highly regarded by his contemporaries that consent was gladly given and he was interred in the north aisle of the Nave in exalted company, beside the scientist Sir John Herschel and close to Sir Isaac Newton.

CHARLES ROBERT DARWIN
BORN 12 FEBRUARY 1809
DIED 19 APRIL 1882

JOANNES HERSCHEL
GULIELMI HERSCHEL
NATV OPERE FAMA
FILIVS VNICVS
"COELIS EXPLORATIS"
HIC PROPE NEWTONUM
REQUIESCIT

O ET GENERATIO
RABUNT

HEIRESS APPARENT

ANGELA BURDETT-COUTTS (d 1906)

When the second wife of the late banking partner Thomas Coutts died, in 1837, Thomas's youngest grandchild inherited a fortune and a half share in the Coutts' banking empire. At the age of 23 Angela Burdett became one of the richest women in the country. As a stipulation of the will she took the name Coutts and subsequently embarked upon a life of high society and charitable giving.

Burdett-Coutts led something of a double life; she entertained the upper echelons of London society at her country home in Highgate by night, but by day she was busy setting up soup kitchens and organising social housing schemes for the deprived in the East End. She sought the advice of her close friend Charles Dickens and together they founded the Urania Cottage for fallen women. Burdett-Coutts was greatly influenced by the plight of many of Dickens' literary characters and in response to *Oliver Twist* she helped to found the Ragged Schools Union in 1844, which led to the establishment of hundreds of schools offering free education to disadvantaged children. She became known to many as the 'Queen of the poor'. In recognition of their friendship Dickens dedicated his novel *Martin Chuzzlewit* to her.

The philanthropic interests of Burdett-Coutts were many and varied and much of her work was carried out anonymously. She maintained the Brompton Cancer Hospital, founded the Royal Marsden Hospital and helped the Irish with relief centres during the Great Potato Famine; she was an enthusiastic supporter of the RSPCA and the NSPCC as well as the British Horological Institute; she acted as President of the British Beekeepers Association and patron of the British Goat Society; she donated four of the twelve bells at St Paul's Cathedral, funded the construction of churches and provided for colonial missionary work to Africa whilst also funding Livingstone's explorations in central Africa; she bestowed lifeboats in Plymouth, Margate and Brittany and drinking fountains in London parks for dogs as well as humans, and she also established the Columbia Road market in Hackney. Her benevolence knew no bounds and in her lifetime it is thought she had given away more than £3million, which is the equivalent to about £250million in today's money.

As such an eligible and powerful woman she attracted many suitors, but none succeeded; instead she fell in love with and proposed to the elderly Duke of Wellington who was more than twice her age. He declined, but at the age of 67 she caused quite a scandal by marrying her American-born assistant, who was half her age. In doing so she also forfeited much of her inheritance as her Grandmother's will stipulated that she should not marry a foreigner.

In 1871 Queen Victoria honoured her with a peerage and the title Baroness Burdett-Coutts of Highgate and Brookfield, in recognition of her immense charitable contribution to society, but she had no children and the title died with her when she passed away at the age of 92. Her body lay in state at her home in Piccadilly and many thousands passed through to pay their respects. She was buried beneath a simple stone by the West Door in the nave of Westminster Abbey.

BURIED AMONG THE KINGS

THE UNKNOWN WARRIOR (d 1918)

The concept of a tomb for an Unknown Warrior was first put forward in 1916 by an army chaplain, Reverend David Railton, who had seen a simple grave on the Western Front with a wooden cross bearing the hand written inscription, 'An Unknown British Soldier'. The idea gathered pace with MPs and the Prime Minister at the time, David Lloyd George, supported the notion. The sheer weight of public feeling eventually convinced King George V that giving an unidentified British soldier a state funeral at Westminster Abbey would act as a symbolic honour to the hundreds of thousands who lost their lives on the battlefields of Northern Europe and across the British Empire during the First World War.

As the second anniversary of Armistice Day approached, a committee was dispatched to France. The bodies of four unidentified British soldiers were exhumed from four different battle sites, the Somme, Arras, Ypres and Aisne. The four were brought together at a military chapel at Saint-Pol where the commander of British troops in France, Brigadier General LJ Wyatt, picked one at random. The body was placed in a coffin and transported to Boulogne, the others were reburied.

Before crossing the channel to Dover the coffin was placed inside another which had been specially made from the timbers of an oak felled in the garden of Hampton Court Palace. This was sealed with iron bands and topped with a medieval sword from the Royal Collection; it was then covered with a Union flag supplied by the Reverend Railton.

The casket journeyed by train from Dover to Victoria Station, and on the morning of 11 November 1920 it was placed on to a horse drawn Royal Artillery gun carriage to be solemnly carried through the streets of the capital in front of huge crowds of hushed onlookers. As the cortege processed from Victoria to the Abbey it passed the Cenotaph war memorial on Whitehall which was unveiled by the King. The Royal family then followed the carriage to the west entrance of the Abbey where it was received by a guard of honour of one hundred Victoria Cross recipients.

The coffin was interred in soil collected from the battlefields of France and finished with a slab of black Belgian marble. The inscription, which was written by the Dean of Westminster and engraved in brass from melted down munitions, begins 'Beneath this stone rests the body of a British Warrior unknown by name or rank, brought from France to lie among the most illustrious of the land', and features a passage from *Chronicles* 'They buried him among the kings, because he had done good toward God and toward his house'. Such was the impact of the event that in the following week more than a million people visited the tomb. It remains the only floor tomb within the vast mausoleum of Westminster Abbey that it is forbidden to walk upon.

In 1923, following her marriage to Prince Albert, later George VI, Elizabeth Bowes-Lyon the Queen Mother laid her wedding bouquet on the tomb as a poignant tribute to her brother Fergus who died on the Western Front in 1915. The practice has continued as an accepted Royal Wedding tradition at the Abbey and recently the bouquet of the Duchess of Cambridge was placed here in 2011, following her marriage to Prince William.

SIR
HENRY IRVING
1838-1905
1907
LAURENCE
OLIVIER
O·M·ACTOR
1989
DAVID
BORN 20TH
DIED 20TH
EVA MARIA
BORN 29TH
DIED

TO BE, OR NOT TO BE

LAURENCE OLIVIER (d 1989)

Laurence Olivier is widely regarded as one of the greatest actors of the 20th century. He was born in Dorking, Surrey, to a strict High Anglican minister and a loving mother who died when he was only 12. His mother had great hopes for her youngest child and her last words were reputed to have been "Darling Larry, no matter what your father says, be an actor. Be a great actor. For me."

Olivier went on to establish one of the most significant stage careers of his generation with dozens of Shakespeare productions under his belt, most notably alongside the likes of Ralph Richardson and Alec Guinness at the Old Vic before the War and then at the New Theatre after the Old Vic suffered bomb damage in the Blitz.

Although Olivier felt much more at home on the stage, he enjoyed a hugely successful movie career. He starred in his first film role in 1930s *The Temporary Widow* and went on to act in more than sixty movies, becoming one of the most Oscar-nominated actors ever.

Olivier's famous relationship with Vivien Leigh began in 1937 after they were cast together in the film *Fire Over England*. They both travelled to Hollywood in 1939, where Olivier was to star as Heathcliff in *Wuthering Heights* and Leigh as Scarlett O'Hara in *Gone with the Wind*. Their relationship blossomed and both were made stars by their respective films, each earning an Oscar nomination.

During World War II Olivier served in the Royal Navy Fleet Air Arm as a pilot but was never called to action. It has been suggested that he was recruited as an undercover agent in the United States for the British government on the instructions of Winston Churchill, but the claims are unsubstantiated.

Olivier enjoyed tremendous critical acclaim and was assured of Hollywood stardom following his next roles in Alfred Hitchcock's *Rebecca*, and as Mr Darcy in *Pride and Prejudice*. This success allowed him to indulge his passion for Shakespeare. He starred in and directed adaptations of *Henry V*, *Richard III* and *Hamlet*, for which he won two Oscars, making him the first actor to have directed himself in an Oscar-winning performance. Olivier was also the first person to be nominated for an acting Oscar across five decades, between the 30s and the 70s.

He founded the National Theatre Company in 1963 and became its first artistic director at the Old Vic, whilst construction of a new National Theatre took place on the South Bank. In their opening production Olivier directed Peter O'Toole as Hamlet and went on to direct many other productions as well as appearing in a further 12 plays during his tenure. Construction of the National Theatre complex was completed in 1976 and the main auditorium was named the 'Olivier' in his honour.

He was knighted in 1947, made a life peer in 1970, and was awarded the Order of Merit in 1981, but he always retained a sense of modesty; when asked if he should be addressed as Lord Olivier or Sir Laurence, he would reply, "Call me Larry".

Olivier died at his home in Sussex on 11 July 1989 and was buried at Westminster Abbey under the same roof as some of the historical figures he brought to the screen, such as Henry V, General John Burgoyne (in *The Devil's Disciple*) and Air Chief Marshal Hugh Dowding (in *The Battle of Britain*). Olivier spoke at his own memorial service, a first for the Abbey, when a recording of an extract from *Henry V* was played to the congregation.

His ashes were interred in Poets Corner beneath a simple stone of Westmorland green slate, beside the graves of the great actors David Garrick and Sir Henry Irving and beneath a memorial to William Shakespeare.

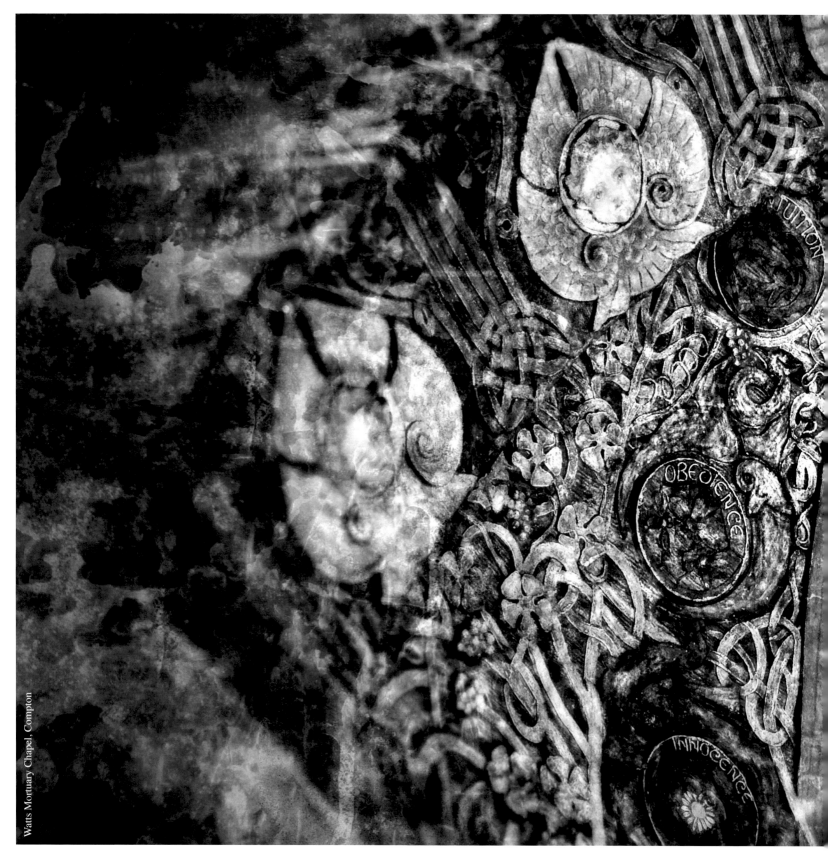

Watts Mortuary Chapel, Compton

HOME
COUNTIES

STATE OF THE NATION

WILLIAM PENN (d 1718)

William Penn was born to the Royal Navy Admiral and politician Sir William Penn. Admiral Penn had great hopes for young William but was bitterly disappointed when Penn became close friends with the Quaker founder, George Fox, and he converted to the Religious Society of Friends.

Penn suffered a great deal of persecution for his beliefs and this culminated with his trial in 1670, charged with unlawful assembly and sedition. The judge was eager to find Penn guilty and put pressure on the jury, even going so far as starving them, but when they returned a 'not guilty' verdict he found the jury in contempt of court and sent them all to prison. The members of the jury battled for their freedom and in doing so they achieved a landmark ruling by which all juries were independent and free from the control of judges. It was largely due to the persecution suffered by Penn and his Quaker brethren that he was prompted to establish a new Quaker settlement in North America.

Penn's father had played a role in restoring King Charles II to the throne by helping to return the King from exile in the Netherlands, and some years after his death Penn received the repayment of a debt that the King owed his father. In 1681 the King granted Penn a vast area of land, some 45,000 square miles to the west and south of New Jersey and Penn led a mass emigration of Buckinghamshire Quakers.

Penn named the land 'Sylvania', Latin for 'woodland', but, much to his embarrassment, it was the King who decided to prefix this with 'Penn' as an honour to his father. Penn also named the area in which he settled 'Bucks County' after his Buckinghamshire home in England. He introduced a 'Frame of Government' in 1682, which set out many of the democratic principles that would go on to influence the United States Constitution, including the concept of 'amendments' which allowed laws to evolve as times changed.

His charter declared that all colonists would be granted religious freedom, which was particularly appealing to those who had suffered from persecution in their respective homelands. Minorities such as Catholics, Jews, Amish Mennonites and Huguenots crossed the Atlantic from Europe to seek a better life.

Further lands were secured by Penn, not by subduing the local tribes but by diplomacy and good business, and he founded the city of Philadelphia, naming it after the Greek for 'philos' (love) and 'adelphos' (brother), 'brotherly love'. Penn had planned to settle in Philadelphia but severe financial mismanagement forced him to return to England in 1701 where he faced an uncertain future as well as a spell in a debtors' prison. He was stricken with a stroke in 1712 which left him unable to speak or look after himself.

He died penniless in 1718 and was buried in a family plot in front of the Quaker meeting house near to the 'Mayflower Barn' in Jordans, which was reputedly built from the timbers of the ship that carried the Pilgrim fathers to the New World in 1620. Not surprisingly, both sites now prove to be popular tourist destinations for visiting Americans with an interest in the founding of their nation.

DOWN THE RABBIT HOLE

LEWIS CARROLL (d 1898)

The Adventures of Alice in Wonderland have captivated audiences for a century and half, from the first manuscript given by Lewis Carroll to Alice herself in 1864, to Tim Burton's computer-animated 3D cinema release in 2010, the story has lost none of its appeal and remains one of the most popular children's books ever written.

It all began in 1862 when the Reverend Charles Lutwidge Dodgson took the daughters of his friend Henry Liddell, the Vice-Chancellor of Oxford University, for a boat trip along the Thames. To pass the time Dodgson made up a story, about a little girl who is sat on the riverbank with her sister when she sees a talking rabbit run by with a pocket watch and, in the spirit of adventure, she decides to follow him down a rabbit hole. The three young girls loved the story, especially the 10-year-old Alice Liddell, who asked if he would write the story down for her. Dodgson obliged and as a Christmas gift in 1864 he presented Alice with a handwritten manuscript of *Alice's Adventures Under Ground* complete with illustrations he had drawn himself.

The book attracted an enthusiastic response from the children of Dodgson's friends and he was encouraged to find a publisher. *Alice's Adventures in Wonderland* was first printed in 1865 under the pseudonym Lewis Carroll. Initially the book wasn't particularly well received but it soon developed momentum when he wrote a sequel *Through the Looking-Glass, and What Alice Found There* in 1871. Alice became a global phenomenon and it made Lewis Carroll a household name. The book is so revered even now that in 1998, at an auction marking the 100th anniversary of Carroll's death, one of only six surviving 1865 editions of *Alice's Adventures in Wonderland*, sold for a record $1.54 million, making it the most expensive children's book ever sold.

Dodgson was also a well-respected mathematician; he taught geometry and algebra for many years at Christ Church College and wrote extensive scholarly texts on the subject. He was fascinated by puzzles, cryptography and playing games with logic and much of his nonsense poetry and fictional writing contained elements of this. Another great passion of his was photography and he became something of a professional when it was still a relatively difficult new art form. Dodgson mastered a technique known as the 'wet collodian' process which involved coating and exposing glass negatives and making paper 'albumen' prints using egg whites. He produced in the region of 3000 images, many of which were portraits of children and members of his family, but he also photographed some of the great names of Victorian society such as Rossetti, Faraday and Tennyson.

The death of his father in 1868 left Charles, as the oldest son, the head of the family. With his new found responsibility and growing wealth he bought a home in Guildford for his six unmarried sisters. Dodgson himself never married or had children and he spent his remaining days in Guildford with his sisters. He died of pneumonia in the winter of 1898, shortly before his 66th birthday, and was buried by his family in a basic plot with a simple monument at Mount Cemetery to the south of Guildford, on a hill overlooking the town.

INTO AFRICA
HENRY MORTON STANLEY (d 1904)

There can't be many people whose fame almost entirely rests on a quotation but, despite his legacy as one of the great Victorian adventurers, Henry Morton Stanley is largely remembered for uttering the immortal words, "Doctor Livingstone, I presume?" on discovering the explorer, presumed lost during an expedition to find the source of the Nile, deep in the African continent.

Born John Rowlands in Wales, he had spent his childhood in a workhouse for the poor, but in 1859, aged 18, Rowlands immigrated to America, landing in New Orleans. He found employment with a trader by the name of Henry Hope Stanley who became something of father to him, so much so that Rowlands took his name and adopted a new identity.

Henry Morton Stanley fought with the Confederate Army and later joined the Navy before taking up a career in journalism. In 1868 he joined the staff of the *New York Herald* and made his first foray into Africa when he was assigned to report on the war in Abyssinia (now Ethiopia). The following year, as a valued overseas correspondent, Stanley was sent on a high profile, well-funded mission to find the elusive British explorer David Livingstone in the heart of Africa. Stanley set off in 1871 from the island of Zanzibar and his seven-month expedition took him 700 hundreds miles through dense jungle to the shores of Lake Tanganyika.

Stanley found Livingstone at the town of Ujiji in poor health and dangerously low on supplies. It is suggested that Stanley's famous greeting was regarded as tongue in cheek as they were the only white men to be found for hundreds of miles. The two men spent four months with one another and made further explorations to establish that there was no link between Lake Tanganyika and the River Nile. Within 18 months of their parting, Livingstone had died of malaria. Stanley published an account of his trip in the book *How I Found Livingstone*.

The *Herald* then commissioned Stanley to cover the Anglo-Ashanti War of 1873 in modern day Ghana, but his relationship with the continent was only just beginning. Stanley would spend the next 15 years exploring much of Equatorial Africa and he wrote of his experiences in the book *Through the Dark Continent*. He was sponsored to conduct a trans-Africa expedition that took him from Zanzibar on the east coast to the mouth of the Congo River on the west. He circumnavigated Lake Victoria and was able to confirm John Speke's assertion that the outflow at Ripon Falls on the Lake's northern shore was the source of the Nile. He was also employed by King Leopold II of Belgium from 1879 to 1884 to establish interests in the Congo region, but this largely amounted to cheating native tribal leaders out of their lands. Belgian colonial rule of Congo Free State was blighted by unconscionable atrocities against the Congolese and the people of the DRC today regard both Stanley and Leopold with contempt.

On leaving Africa Stanley discovered that his American fiancée, Alice, had married another man in his absence so he returned to Britain instead of his adopted homeland. He became an MP, for Lambeth North, was awarded a knighthood and bought an estate in Pirbright in 1899. His grave is marked by a large granite monolith at the entrance to St Michael's churchyard and is inscribed with the words 'Bula Mutari', which translate from the Kongo language as 'stone breaker', a name he earned whilst building a road in the Congo.

THE ART OF SHOPPING

ARTHUR LIBERTY (d 1917)

Liberty & Co is one of the capital's most famous shopping institutions, known around the world for its eclectic design and distinctive style, and it was the unique vision of the man who gave it his name, Arthur Lasenby Liberty.

Liberty moved from his home town of Chesham to work in Regent Street where he became manager of 'Farmer and Roger's' Oriental Warehouse, but after ten years he left his job and secured a £2000 loan from his father in law to start up his own business.

Having gained an invaluable education in oriental arts and crafts he applied this experience to his own store where he specialised in selling Eastern ornaments and fabrics. In 1875 he took out a lease on half a shop at 218a Regent Street and within 18 months he had repaid the loan and acquired the other half of the shop. As his empire expanded he began to occupy the neighbouring buildings too.

Part of Liberty's great skill was to identify trends and to adjust his business accordingly. He realised that imported fabrics from the Far East were too delicate and couldn't be used by dressmakers or furnishers, so he enlisted the help of some innovative British designers and began to manufacture his own fabrics. He also addressed the high production costs of fine hand-crafted metal-ware and released his own range of jewellery and home-ware for the mass market by using automated die-casting methods. Liberty embraced the Aesthetic Movement

and commissioned work from some of the finest avant-garde designers of the day. By encouraging the talents of new artists, Liberty placed his store at the forefront of the Art Nouveau movement. Liberty & Co attracted a discerning clientele and became world renowned for its powerful and modern design, in Italy, especially, Art Nouveau was referred to as 'Liberty Style'.

The iconic mock Tudor premises that stand today on Great Marlborough Street were completed in 1924, seven years after the death of Liberty, and were built from the timbers of two of the last wooden Royal Navy warships, *HMS Impregnable* and *HMS Hindostan*. The Liberty family removed the ship's figurehead of Admiral Lord Howe from *Impregnable*, and placed it near the family home in the village of Lee in the Chiltern Hills, where it remains a somewhat bizarre addition to the landscape.

With his new found wealth Liberty returned to the area of his childhood and bought the manor house and estate at The Lee in 1898. As Lord of the Manor he did a great deal to improve the surrounding area and made additions to the village itself, such as building cottages and pubs, pumping fresh water from the valley below, laying out a village green and cricket pitch, as well as making improvements to the village church of St John the Baptist, where he is now buried.

His splendid gravestone, in the form of a Celtic cross, was designed by Liberty & Co.'s most famous Art Nouveau designer, Archibald Knox.

GOLFING FOR GOLD

SAMUEL RYDER (d 1936)

Samuel Ryder was the instigator of one of sport's greatest rivalries. The Ryder Cup started out as a friendly transatlantic golfing tournament and 'lunch party' but it has since grown to become the highest profile sporting contest of its kind in the world. The lucrative event now generates millions in revenue from television rights and sponsorship deals but the players do not receive any prize money, competing only for national pride and bragging rights.

Ryder made his fortune after setting up in business from his garden shed in St Albans with the perfectly simple idea of selling penny packets of garden seeds via mail order. The business enjoyed rapid growth, moved to new premises and went on to employ more than a hundred people.

Ryder became a workaholic, he was heavily involved with the local church and he also served as a councillor and mayor of St Albans, but when his health began to suffer a friend suggested he take up golf as the fresh air would do him good. Being more interested in cricket, he was reluctant at first but eventually gave it a go.

At 50 years of age he'd come to the sport relatively late in life, but Ryder applied a similar determination as he had to his business. He employed the golf professional Abe Mitchell to instruct him for an enormous annual fee of £1000; he practised almost every day and it wasn't long before he played off an enviable single figure handicap. Ryder became captain of Verulam Golf Club in St Albans and began to sponsor local events, which ultimately led to his interest in pairing teams from the UK and United States.

Ryder donated the famous gold trophy and the inaugural Ryder Cup was staged at Worcester Country Club, Massachusetts, in 1927. The figure that adorns the lid of the trophy is that of Ryder's golfing coach and friend Abe Mitchell, who was to captain the British team at the first Ryder Cup match but was forced to pull out due to illness. That first contest was won by the United States team who were led by the great Walter Hagen.

The prestigious tournament has been hosted every other year on alternating sides of the Atlantic ever since, except during the Second World War. Up until the 1985 competition the US team had dominated the honours, winning all but three matches (at one stage they had remained unbeaten for 28 years), but from 1979 players from continental Europe were invited to play and, under the captaincy of Tony Jacklin, the tables were finally turned. The European team has claimed the majority of wins since.

Ryder died at the Langham Hotel on Portland Place in January 1936, at the age of 77, and was buried at Hatfield Road Cemetery in St Albans with his favourite golf club, a five iron known as a 'mashie'.

FUTURE IMPERFECT
ALDOUS HUXLEY (d 1963)

In the sleepy Surrey village of Compton there can be found one of the most picturesque cemeteries in the country. When the village ran out of burial space at the local churchyard in 1895 and land for a new cemetery was purchased nearby, the distinguished artist George Frederic Watts and his wife Mary offered to build a chapel at their own expense. They enlisted the help of more than 70 villagers and together crafted the decorative mortuary chapel, a stunning example of Arts and Crafts architecture, with a spectacular Celtic Art Nouveau interior.

Overlooking the Watts Mortuary Chapel lies the grave of the Huxley family, the best known of whom is the writer Aldous Huxley. Huxley's literary breakthrough came in 1932 with the publication of his dystopian masterpiece *Brave New World*, a nightmarish 'negative utopia' of a globalised future. Set in 2540AD, the book tells the story of a totalitarian 'World State' that has created a homogenised yet harmonious global society, however the irony of this existence is that society has lost touch with the very idea of religion and culture, a chilling utopia with no sympathy or empathy.

Although it was intended as a piece of satirical fiction, *Brave New World* has proved to be somewhat prophetic. Huxley wrote that we appeared to be accelerating towards this alternative future faster than he had ever imagined. The book was banned in Ireland on its release for being anti-religion and it still remains controversial; in 2010 the American Library Association revealed that Brave New World was still shocking audiences to this day and named it among its top ten most complained about books.

Huxley moved to Los Angeles in 1937 and worked for a short time writing screenplays for MGM, earning credits in the writing of Hollywood adaptations of *Pride and Prejudice* and *Jane Eyre*. Although he suffered from considerable blindness for most of his life he was a prolific writer of novels, poetry, short stories and essays, but he is probably best known for his book *The Doors of Perception*, based on his mind-altering experiments with the psychedelic drug Mescaline.

In the 1960s, as experimental drug use became a key part of the burgeoning Californian counterculture, Huxley became an unwilling advocate for hallucinogenic drugs such as LSD. His lasting popularity was secured when his book was cited as the influence behind the name of rock group The Doors.

As he lay dying from throat cancer, Huxley requested that his wife administer a dose of LSD to ease his passing; she later described his final journey as 'the most beautiful death'. Huxley died on the same day as the author CS Lewis, but any news of their deaths was eclipsed by the assassination of US President John F Kennedy which also occurred on 22 November 1963.

Although Huxley had spent the last 25 years of his life in California, his ashes were repatriated to the village cemetery at Compton. Also interred in the family plot is Huxley's elder brother Julian; who was one of the 20th century's leading biologists, first Director-General of UNESCO and co-founder of the World Wildlife Fund.

THE MAN BEHIND THE MASK
BORIS KARLOFF (d 1969)

The square head, scarred face, dead stare and bolted neck of Frankenstein's Monster remain one of cinema's most iconic images; the face that launched a million Halloween masks. What might seem rather tame by today's standards was, at the time, the epitome of horror. It is testament to the power and pathos of his portrayal that Boris Karloff is now remembered primarily for that one defining role.

The young William Henry Pratt, born in Peckham in 1887, grew up with a lisp and a stutter; not that this did anything to dampen his ambition for acting; he immigrated to North America at the age of 22 and gave himself the exotic name Boris Karloff. Karloff worked hard to establish himself in Hollywood, taking up extra work in silent movies. By the time his big break came with Universal Pictures' loose adaptation of Mary Shelley's Gothic horror story, *Frankenstein*, in 1931, Karloff had already made 75 films. In fact, *Frankenstein* was just one of 15 movies he made that same year.

In the opening credits of the film Karloff was simply billed with a question mark to enhance the mystique of the monster. The studio was also keen to build this suspense as Bela Lugosi was originally scheduled to play the part following his success in *Dracula*. Lugosi had pulled out of the project when he realised the monster would not be a speaking part. Director James Whale brought in the unknown Karloff as his replacement.

The movie is considered a classic of early Horror. Many adaptations have been made since and, although it is not faithful to Shelley's novel, this version remains the original and best.

Karloff had established himself as the face of horror, going on to star as *The Mummy* and *The Ghoul* as well as stepping into Frankenstein's considerable shoes for two sequels *The Bride of…* and *The Son of Frankenstein*.

Between 1934 and 1945 Karloff appeared in a spell of horror double headers with his rival Bela Lugosi, in the Edgar Allen Poe adaptations *The Black Cat* and *The Raven* and Robert Louis Stevenson's *Body Snatcher*, amongst others. Karloff was considered the bigger star and although Lugosi acted some of the lead roles, Karloff invariably received top billing, causing some friction between them. The two giants of horror never became close friends but they always retained a respectful professionalism.

Karloff enjoyed a varied career and maintained a run of high profile roles, not only in horror movies but also on stage and television. Even into old age and confined to a wheelchair Karloff could not stop working; his last three movies were released posthumously. He is honoured with two stars on the Hollywood Walk of Fame for his significant contribution to the motion picture and television industries.

With failing health Karloff returned to the UK to live out his retirement. He succumbed to pneumonia after catching a chill and was cremated at Guildford Crematorium in Godalming; his ashes were laid to rest in the Garden of Remembrance. A commemorative rose bush exists, although his plaque has gone missing. The tributes left by visiting fans are now all that mark his plot.

THE SWINDON SIREN

DIANA DORS (d 1984)

Diana Fluck took the name 'Dors' from her maternal grandmother when she signed an acting contract with the Rank Organisation. She appeared in her first film in 1947 and in post-war Britain the glamorous starlet was a tonic for a depressed nation. When Marilyn Monroe made her name in the 1950 film *The Asphalt Jungle* a comparison was made between the two that would see Dors referred to as the British answer to Monroe.

Dors was just 15 years old when she was paid the handsome salary of £10 per day for her two weeks filming with Richard Attenborough in *Dancing with Crime*, earning the equivalent of more than £5000 in today's money. She carried the cash home in a suitcase to her disbelieving parents. Her star rose quickly and in 1948 Dors appeared in six films, the most notable of which was in the timeless Dickens adaptation of *Oliver Twist*. She was only 21 when she was registered as the youngest owner of a Rolls-Royce in the UK. Dors proved beyond a shadow of doubt that she had great acting talent, but she was largely promoted as a sex symbol and there followed a succession of supporting roles in which she played the voluptuous and brassy screen siren.

In 1951 Dors played a starring role in *Lady Godiva Rides Again* which featured Joan Collins in her movie debut and also Ruth Ellis, who would become well known as the last woman to be executed in England after murdering her husband. Just a year after Ellis's execution Dors played one of her most acclaimed roles, starring as a woman who is sentenced to hang for murder in *Yield to the Night*.

Dors had a rocky personal life which saw her married three times; she tied the knot with Dennis Hamilton within weeks of their meeting but the marriage ended with his death in 1959, her second, to American comedian and TV host Richard Dawson, lasted just seven years and ended in recriminations and bankruptcy, and it was only with her third marriage, to actor Richard Lake in 1968, that she found some stability, although this was not a particularly trouble free union either. Dors became the subject of tabloid exposés for her extravagant lifestyle and tales of her 'adult' celebrity parties led to much criticism, even the Archbishop of Canterbury condemned her as a 'wayward hussy'.

Throughout the sixties and seventies Dors continued to appear in movies but focused her efforts on television work and cabaret performance. She starred in British horror b-movies such as *Theatre of Blood* and *From Beyond the Grave* and also in titillating, low-budget sex comedies such as *Adventures of a Taxi Driver* and *Keep It Up Downstairs* but she became known to a new generation when she played the Fairy Godmother in the Adam and the Ants music video for 'Prince Charming' in 1981.

Diana Dors was a genuine national treasure and when she succumbed to ovarian cancer at the age of 52 the nation mourned an icon. She was buried at Sunningdale Catholic Cemetery wearing a gold lame evening gown. Lake struggled to come to terms with her death and less than six months later he took his own life with a shotgun and was buried beside her.

Following her death a tantalising mystery emerged, Dors had given one of her sons a coded message that would reputedly unlock the whereabouts of a secret £2 million fortune. The message, which had been encrypted using a 16th century Vigenere alphabetic cipher, was finally decoded in 2003 but unfortunately the vital password to explain its meaning was known only by her husband and any chance of tracing the money disappeared with his suicide.

SCRUMDIDDLYUMPTIOUS

ROALD DAHL (d 1990)

It is not often that a famous grave becomes a point of pilgrimage for children but in the village of Great Missenden there lies the author Roald Dahl, his grave awash with drawings from children who have been inspired by his writings. Occasionally macabre, often wildly exaggerated, but always funny, Dahl's books have been delighting children for many years and will do for generations to come.

Dahl was born in Wales to Norwegian parents and from a young age he craved adventure. At the age of 18 he took a job with Shell Oil that would send him to the far flung corners of the world. At the outbreak of World War II Dahl was working in Tanganyika in East Africa (now Tanzania). He joined the Royal Air Force in Nairobi and spent six months training to be a fighter pilot in Iraq. But in 1940 he nearly lost his life when he was forced to crash land in Libya. He suffered a fractured skull and was temporarily blinded, but after just five months of recovery, he was back in the pilot's seat flying sorties in Greece and Palestine.

Following his airborne heroics Dahl was re-assigned to New York where he took up a post with the British Security Coordination (BSC), a secret underground network of spies and propagandists set up by MI6 who would use their charm and wit to influence American political opinion and persuade the media to support the Allies in Europe. During this time Flight Lieutenant Dahl wrote his first children's book *The Gremlins* for Walt Disney, about mischievous creatures that would sabotage British aircraft. He gave a copy to First Lady Eleanor Roosevelt who read it to her grandchildren; they loved the book so much Dahl was invited to the White House for dinner with the President. Among his colleagues in New York was the naval officer Ian Fleming. Dahl and Fleming were close friends and in 1967 Dahl was chosen to write the screenplay for the fifth James Bond film *You Only Live Twice* despite having little experience in writing screenplays. Dahl was also called upon to write a musical adaptation to another of Fleming's novels *Chitty Chitty Bang Bang* for which he created the character The Child Catcher.

Dahl returned to England after the war and began to write professionally. His imaginative style and vivid characters earned him legions of avid readers young and old. In 1961 *James and the Giant Peach* marked his new beginning as a successful children's author, and he cemented his reputation with *Charlie and the Chocolate Factory* in 1964.

Dahl's stories combined the grotesque with the comical and it was his work with illustrator Quentin Blake on the books *The Enormous Crocodile* and *The Twits* that they were really brought to life. Blake's joyful illustrative style came to define Dahl's characters and there followed a long and fruitful partnership.

Dahl's books always lent themselves well to the screen and there have been many successful adaptations which include *Matilda* (1996), *The Witches* (1990), *Fantastic Mr Fox* (2009), *The BFG* (1989) and the timeless classic *Willy Wonka & the Chocolate Factory* (1971), starring Gene Wilder, for which Dahl also wrote the screenplay.

Dahl's famous writing shed, where he wrote many of his best loved stories, remained untouched since his death and for over 20 years it had been left to decay, but in 2011 it was the subject of a £500,000 preservation campaign. The entire contents and furnishings of the writing hut were moved piece by piece and the display now forms the centrepiece to the Roald Dahl Museum and Story Centre which opened in 2005 in Great Missenden.

A GIRL CALLED DUSTY

DUSTY SPRINGFIELD (d 1999)

Mary Isobel Catherine Bernadette O'Brien was born to an Irish Catholic family in west London and went on to become one of the most highly respected and best loved British female singers of all time. As a Sixties icon Dusty Springfield became known for her exceptional soulful voice and was immediately recognisable by her distinctive peroxide beehive hairstyle and heavy panda-eyed make up.

The young Mary O'Brien joined a folk singing group with her elder brother, Dionysius, and Tim Feild; Dion and Mary adopted the surname Springfield, as a play on their band mate's surname, and gave themselves the Christian names Tom and Dusty. The Springfields enjoyed moderate success in the early 1960s in the UK and United States, but it was when the group disbanded and Dusty went solo that the star was truly born.

Dusty Springfield's first single 'I Only Want to Be with You' was released at the end of 1963, just weeks after the demise of The Springfields, and it catapulted her to the top 5 of the UK charts and into the US Billboard chart. She performed the song on the first edition of the new music TV show *Top of the Pops* alongside The Rolling Stones and The Beatles.

Her first solo album *A Girl Called Dusty* in 1964 featured the tracks 'Twenty Four Hours from Tulsa' and 'Anyone Who Had a Heart' which were written by the legendary hit-makers Burt Bacharach and Hal David. This signalled the start of a successful spell with the songwriters that culminated in her recording 'The Look of Love' which featured in the James Bond parody *Casino Royale,* starring Peter Sellers, and was nominated for an Academy Award for Best Song. Her only British number one single came in 1966 with the soaring anti-love ballad that came to define her sound and style 'You Don't Have to Say You Love Me'.

In an effort to get closer to the roots of her R&B influences Springfield moved to the United States to record the classic soul album *Dusty In Memphis* which featured her iconic single 'Son of a Preacher Man'. During this time she recommended to her label bosses at Atlantic Records that they should sign up her friend's new band. The friend was John Paul Jones, and without even hearing a song they offered Led Zeppelin a record deal on Springfield's say so.

Springfield remained in the US recording albums and releasing singles but her career was going into decline and during the 1970s she struggled with drink and drug addiction as well as suffering from depression and insecurities about her sexuality. She achieved chart success once more with the Pet Shop Boys' 'What Have I Done to Deserve This?' and in 1988, with a renewed vigour and a new generation of fans, she moved back to the UK to record a comeback album.

During the recording of her final record in 1995 Springfield was diagnosed with breast cancer. After treatment the cancer went into remission, but by the following year it had returned. She was awarded an OBE in the 1999 New Year Honours list and was expected to receive the award in March at Buckingham Palace, but due to her worsening health the Queen allowed for the medal to be presented in a private gathering at her hospital bedside in January. She passed away at her home in Henley-on-Thames just two months later. Hundreds of mourners gathered and the town came to a standstill for her funeral at St Mary the Virgin Church.

MR MOONLIGHT
FRANKIE VAUGHAN (d 1999)

Frankie Vaughan was one of the best loved British family entertainers of the post war period and will always be remembered as the suave, high-kicking crooner with a sharp dress sense. He was born Frank Abelson in Liverpool and acquired the stage name Vaughan from his Russian grandmother, who would refer to him as her number 'vorn' grandson.

He recorded his first single in 1950 and hits such as 'Give Me The Moonlight Give Me The Girl' in 1955, 'The Green Door' in 1956, 'Kisses Sweeter than Wine' and his first number one 'The Garden of Eden' in 1957 propelled him to stardom in the UK, but Vaughan's brand of traditional pop would soon be eclipsed by the chart success of Elvis Presley and a new generation of pop music. However Vaughan continued to record music throughout the 60s and 70s, becoming one of British television's most popular variety singers. During his lifetime he released more than 80 singles and it was the song 'Give Me the Moonlight' that became a signature tune.

Vaughan was performing in Las Vegas when he was approached to star with Marilyn Monroe in the 1960 musical comedy *Let's Make Love*. Although the film was not considered a success for Monroe, it represented the pinnacle of Vaughan's brief film career. During filming Vaughan was apparently innocent to the advances of his sex symbol co-star, but his wife Stella was not quite so trusting of Monroe, and chastened by his experience in Hollywood the loving husband turned his back on a movie career to return to his wife in England. No-one could separate them, not even Marilyn Monroe. Such was his devotion for Stella that, in 48 years of marriage, he never once removed his wedding ring and that whilst filming it had to be covered up.

When he was evacuated during the war Vaughan joined the Lancaster Lad's Club, where he had early aspirations of becoming a boxer. But in later life as a successful entertainer he became a tireless charity worker, supporting youth projects and donating royalties from many of his hit singles to the National Association of Boy's Clubs.

In the late sixties Vaughan played a concert at the Glasgow Pavilion, but he was so shocked by the level of violence and gang warfare in the Easterhouse area of the city, that he met with gang leaders to organise a weapons amnesty. He donated the proceeds from his concert to set up the Easterhouse Project, which continues to help the youth of today in such a deprived area.

Following a succession of operations Vaughan succumbed to heart failure at the age of 71 and was buried in a traditional Jewish ceremony at Bushey Jewish Cemetery near Watford.

BEST OF BRITISH

SIR JOHN MILLS (d 2005)

John Mills was one of the best loved British actors of the 20th century. He came to personify the quintessentially English 'stiff upper lip', decent, patriotic and good humoured. He didn't have screen idol looks, but was dashing enough to make a convincing hero.

Mills made his screen debut in the 1932 comedy feature *The Midshipmaid*. It took him some years, working his way up the bill in a variety of roles, before landing his first lead in *Brown on Resolution* a 1935 adaptation of CS Forester's World War I novel in which he played the first of many war heroes. In 1939 he made his first Hollywood studio feature for MGM alongside Robert Donat and Greer Garson in *Goodbye, Mr Chips*.

World War II seemingly brought a halt to Mills' acting career as he joined the Royal Engineers, but soon after being commissioned he was declared unfit for service due to an intestinal ulcer. He returned to the screen in Noel Coward's patriotic morale-boosting film *In Which We Serve* as Shorty Blake, a role Coward wrote especially for him. Mills cemented his place in cinema history as the archetypal wartime hero with the films *We Dive at Dawn* and *This Happy Breed*.

It is possible that Mills was in danger of becoming typecast, especially as many of his post-war films such as *The Colditz Story*, *Dunkirk* and *Ice Cold in Alex* followed a similar theme, but he was able to bring different characteristics to many of his roles, displaying a greater range than he is perhaps remembered for. He also interspersed his wartime repertoire with such cinematic classics as the Dickens adaptation *Great Expectations* and David Lean's *Hobson's Choice*.

It took Mills some years to shake off the trademark war hero roles and in 1959 he acted opposite his 12-year-old daughter Hayley in *Tiger Bay*, which won her a BAFTA Award for most promising newcomer. They worked together on three further films as Mills gradually made the transition from leading man to character actor. After four decades on screen he finally won an acting Oscar in 1970 for his supporting role as 'Michael' the village idiot in *Ryan's Daughter*, a role which required him to speak no lines. He was knighted by the queen in 1977.

Mills was almost entirely deaf and blind in 2003 when he made his final performance, a cameo in Stephen Fry's *Bright Young Things*, bringing to an end a career spanning eight decades and 123 films.

Mills enjoyed a long association with the picturesque Buckinghamshire village of Denham, having made many of his earlier films at Alexander Korda's Denham Studios. In 1975 he and his wife Mary bought 'Hill's House' in the heart of the village, which was once owned by Korda and his wife Merle Oberon.

Both in their nineties, the devoted couple reaffirmed their vows at St Mary's church in Denham after sixty years of marriage, and in 2005 Sir John and Lady Mary passed away within a few months of each other. Their modest grave lies close to the home they shared, in St Mary's churchyard.

APPENDIX

NORTH LONDON

THOMAS STAMFORD RAFFLES
St Mary and Christ Church, Church End, Hendon,
NW4 4JT
www.hendonstmary.co.uk
Tube – Hendon Central

JOHN CONSTABLE
St John-at-Hampstead Churchyard, Church Row,
Hampstead,
NW3 6UU
www.hampsteadparishchurch.org.uk
Tube – Hampstead

ELIZABETH SIDDAL/MICHAEL FARADAY/
KARL MARX/ ALEXANDER LITVINENKO/
MALCOLM McLAREN
Highgate Cemetery, Swain's Lane, N6 6PJ
www.highgatecemetery.org
Tube – Highgate or Archway

CORA CRIPPEN
St Pancras Cemetery, High Road, East Finchley,
N2 9AG
Tube – East Finchley

BRAM STOKER/ ANNA PAVLOVA/ SIGMUND
FREUD/ MARC BOLAN
Golders Green Crematorium, Hoop Lane,
Golders Green, NW11 7NL
Tube – Golders Green

WILLIAM BOOTH
Abney Park Cemetery, Stoke Newington High Street,
N16 0LH
www.abney-park.org.uk
National Rail – Stoke Newington

BILLY FURY
Mill Hill Cemetery, Milespit Hill, Mill Hill,
NW7 2RR
Tube – Mill Hill East

AMY WINEHOUSE
Edgwarebury Cemetery, Edgwarebury Lane,
Edgware, HA8 8QP
www.edgwareburycemetery.org.uk
Tube – Edgware

SOUTH LONDON

THOMAS TWINING
St Mary's Church, Church Street, Twickenham,
TW1 3NJ
www.stmarytwick.org.uk
National Rail – Twickenham

EDMOND HALLEY
St Margaret of Antioch, Brandram Road, Lee,
SE13 5EA
www.stmargaretslee.org.uk
National Rail – Blackheath

SPENCER PERCEVAL
St Luke's Church, The Village, Charlton, SE7 8UG
National Rail – Charlton

WILLIAM BLIGH
Garden Museum, Lambeth Palace Rd, SE1 7LB
www.gardenmuseum.org.uk
Tube – Lambeth North

ISABELLA BEETON/ HENRY TATE/ PAUL
JULIUS REUTER/ HIRAM MAXIM
West Norwood Cemetery, Norwood Road, SE27 9JU
www.westnorwoodcemetery.com
National Rail – West Norwood

RICHARD FRANCIS BURTON
St Mary Magdalen Roman Catholic Church, 61
North Worple Way, Mortlake, SW14 8PR
www.stmarymags.org.uk
National Rail – Mortlake

JOSEPH BAZALGETTE
St Mary's Church, 30 St Mary's Road, Wimbledon,
SW19 7BP
www.stmaryswimbledon.org
National Rail – Wimbledon

WG GRACE
Beckenham Cemetery, Elmers End Road,
Beckenham, BR3 4TD
National Rail – Birkbeck

EBENEZER COBB MORLEY
Old Barnes Cemetery, Barnes Common, SW13 0BL
National Rail – Barnes

HOWARD CARTER
Putney Vale Cemetery, Stag Lane, Wimbledon,
SW15 3DZ
Tube – Southfields

WEST LONDON

WILLIAM HOGARTH
St Nicholas Church, Church Street, Chiswick, W4
2PH
www.stnicholaschiswick.org
Tube – Turnham Green

JOHN SNOW/ HENRY COLE/ JOHN WISDEN/
CHIEF LONG WOLF/ EMMELINE PANKHURST
Brompton Cemetery, Fulham Road, SW10 9UG
Tube – Earls Court

ISAMBARD KINGDOM BRUNEL/ CHARLES
BABBAGE
Kensal Green Cemetery, Harrow Road, W10 4RA
www.kensalgreencemetery.com
Tube – Kensal Green

MARY SEACOLE
St Mary's Catholic Cemetery, Harrow Road,
NW10 5NU
Tube – Kensal Green

DAVID SUTCH
Pinner New Cemetery, Pinner Road, HA5 5RH
Tube – North Harrow

EAST LONDON & CITY

RAHERE
St Bartholomew the Great, Cloth Fair, EC1A 7JQ
www.greatstbarts.com
Tube – Barbican

JOHN SMITH
St. Sepulchre Without Newgate Church, Holborn
Viaduct, EC1A 2DQ
www.st-sepulchre.org.uk
Tube – St Paul's

JOHN BUNYAN/ WILLIAM BLAKE
Bunhill Fields, 38 City Rd, EC1Y 1AU
Tube – Old Street

SAMUEL PEPYS
St Olave Church, 8 Hart Street,
EC3R 7NB
www.sanctuaryinthecity.net/St-Olaves
Tube – Tower Hill

JOHN WESLEY
Wesley's Chapel and Leysian Mission,
49 City Rd, EC1Y 1AU
www.wesleyschapel.org.uk
Tube – Old Street

HORATIO NELSON/ JOHN EVERETT MILLAIS
St Paul's Cathedral, St Paul's Church Yard,
EC4M 8AD
www.stpauls.co.uk
Tube – St Paul's

ELIZABETH FRY
Wanstead Quaker Meeting House, Bush Road,
Wanstead, E11 3AU
www.wansteadquakers.gn.apc.org
Tube – Leytonstone

MARY KELLY
St Patrick's Roman Catholic Cemetery, Langthorne
Road, Leytonstone, E11 4HS
Tube – Leyton

BOBBY MOORE
City of London Cemetery, Aldersbrook Road,
Newham, E12 5DQ
National Rail – Manor Park

KRAY TWINS
Chingford Mount Cemetery, Old Church Road,
E4 8BX
National Rail – Chingford

CENTRAL LONDON

GEOFFREY CHAUCER/ APHRA BEHN/
ISAAC NEWTON/CHARLES DICKENS/
CHARLES DARWIN/ ANGELA BURDETT-
COUTTS/THE UNKNOWN WARRIOR/
LAURENCE OLIVIER
Westminster Abbey, Deans Yard, SW1P 3PA
www.westminster-abbey.org
Tube – Westminster

WALTER RALEIGH
St Margaret's Church, St Margaret Street,
SW1P 3JX
www.westminster-abbey.org/st-margarets
Tube – Westminster

JEREMY BENTHAM
University College London, Gower Street,
WC1E 6BT
www.ucl.ac.uk
Tube – Euston Square

JOHN SOANE
St Pancras Old Church, Pancras Rd, NW1 1UL
www.posp.co.uk/old-st-pancras
Tube – Mornington Crescent

JOSEPH GRIMALDI
Joseph Grimaldi Park, Pentonville Road,
N1 9PE
Tube – Kings Cross St Pancras

MARIE TUSSAUD
St Marys Roman Catholic Church,
Cadogan Street, SW3 2QR
www.stmaryscadoganstreet.co.uk
Tube – Sloane Square

HOME COUNTIES

WILLIAM PENN
Jordans Quaker Meeting House, Welders Lane,
Jordans, Bucks,HP9 2SN
www.quaker.org.uk/jordans
National Rail – Seer Green

LEWIS CARROLL
Mount Cemetery, The Mount, Guildford, Surrey,
GU2 4JB
National Rail – Guildford

HENRY STANLEY
St. Michael's Church, Church Lane, Pirbright,
Surrey, GU24 0JE
www.pirbrightchurch.org.uk
National Rail – Brookwood

ARTHUR LIBERTY
St John the Baptist Church, The Lee, Bucks,

HP16 9LZ
National Rail – Great Missenden

SAMUEL RYDER
Hatfield Road Cemetery, Hatfield Road, St Albans,
Herts, AL1 4LU
National Rail – St Albans

ALDOUS HUXLEY
Compton Village Cemetery, Down Lane, Compton,
Surrey, GU3 1EB
www.wattschapel.co.uk
National Rail – Farncombe

BORIS KARLOFF
Guildford Crematorium, New Pond Road,
Godalming, Surrey, GU7 3DB
National Rail – Farncombe

DIANA DORS
Sunningdale Catholic Cemetery, Kiln Lane,
Sunningdale, Berks, SL5 0LT
National Rail – Sunningdale

ROALD DAHL
St Peter and St Paul Church, Church Lane,
Great Missenden, Bucks, HP16 0BA
www.missendenchurch.org.uk
National Rail – Great Missenden

DUSTY SPRINGFIELD
St Mary the Virgin Church, Hart Street,
Henley-on-Thames, Oxfordshire, RG9 2AU
www.stmaryshenley.org.uk
National Rail – Henley-on-Thames

FRANKIE VAUGHAN
Bushey Jewish Cemetery, Little Bushey Lane,
Bushey, Herts, WD23 3TP
National Rail – Bushey

JOHN MILLS
St. Mary's Church, Village Road, Denham,
Middlesex, UB9 5BH
www.stmary-denham.org.uk
National Rail – Denham

INDEX

www.deadfamouslondon.co.uk